Wave after Wave of Pink

Women Warriors Share Tales of the Storm

Copyright 2022 ©

By Pink Sistas Publishing and all featured authors.

Published by

Pink Sistas Inc. Publishing

Curated by: Michael McCartney, Tara L McGuire, and Pink Sistas

Authors

- Tami Marie Starkey
- Sherrida Preciado Gates
- Jennie Vinson
- Leslie Kerwin Myll
- Kortnee Colbry
- Lisa Warzyn
- Tyreanna Hoxer
- Penda Sidibeh
- Erin Challenger
- Annie Hunnicutt
- Paige Hairston
- Becci Owens
- Danielle Cooper
- Tana Haigler
- Andrea Davis
- Jana Hill
- Delo Fercho
- Kerry Farnham
- Lauren Oman
- Deb Hart
- Amber Conner
- Shannon Preston
- Miranda Brennan
- Robyn McManama
- Tara L McGuire
- April Everist
- Christine Terry

Cover Design: Michael McCartney - DezignZ by Soup
www.dezignzbysoup.com
Cover Art: Michael McCartney - DezignZ by Soup
Proof Editing: Meridith Brand, & Tara L. McGuire
Interior Formating and Graphics: Michael McCartney

ISBN: Paperback 978-1-7923-9012-8

All rights reserved. No part of this book may be reproduced in any form or by any electronic or mechanical means, including information storage and retrieval systems, without written permission from the author, with the exception of using brief quotations in a book review.

Printed in USA

Dedication

We dedicate this book to the numerous women who came before us fighting this life changing disease, the many who are fighting it now, the untold numbers who will fight it in the future, and the millions of people who have supported each of us on this journey as we have fought and continue to fight breast cancer.

While breast cancer is a very personal battle it is never fought alone. It has lasting effects on not only the individual, but their families, friends, loved ones and communities.

Every breast cancer diagnosis is also a call to be a warrior. These warriors fight tremendous battles; for their health, quality of life, continued life with those they love, and to advance research in every area. Sharing our stories is one way we can offer support, hope, and inspiration to these amazing warriors.

We all fight for you and with you.
Stay strong sister, you are not alone.

Annie Hunnicutt

Help us to help others through encouragement and support.

Share your story and picture on social media holding your copy of Wave After Wave of Pink using the hashtag #waveafterwaveofpink

Visit our website: www.pinksistas.org

CONTENTS

Dedication...1

Introduction...4

EVERY LIFE HAS A STORY
Tami Marie Starkey...6

CHAMPIONS NEEDED
Sherrida Preciado Gates..12

GIFTS AND SILVER LININGS
Jennie Vinson..22

MY MARATHON
Leslie Kerwin Myll..29

ROLL OF THE DICE
Kortnee Colbry..39

MY STORY
Lisa Warzyn...49

POSITIVITY HEALS
Tyreanna Hoxer...56

CANCER IN THE PANDEMIC
Penda Sidibeh..68

I THOUGHT I WAS PREPARED
Erin Challenger...78

TALK TO YOUR FAMILY
Annie Hunnicutt...83

I DID NOT FEEL SICK
Paige Hairston...91

IS THIS WHAT I THINK IT IS?
Becci Owens..95

IT'S FINE, I'M FINE, EVERYTHING IS FINE!
Danielle Cooper..105

HOW DIAMONDS ARE FORMED
Tana Haigler..117

FINDING OUT I HAD CANCER
Andrea Davis..129
SAVING GRACE
Jana Hill..140
ROLLER COASTER
Delo Fercho...148
I DON'T DO WAIT AND SEE VERY WELL
Kerry Farnham..158
A YEAR TO REMEMBER
Lauren Oman...171
THE STORM
Deb Hart..184
THE CHOICE DOES NOT BELONG TO FATE
Amber Conner...189
WHAT'S YOUR SUPERPOWER?
Shannon Preston...199
IN THE SHADOW
Miranda Brennan..209
CLOTHED IN DIGNITY
Robyn McManama..216
FROM ONE PEAK TO ANOTHER
Tara L McGuire...225
THE MANY REVELATIONS OF "THE BIG C"
April Everist..241
MY METASTATIC BREAST CANCER JOURNEY!
Christine Terry..249

Thank You Fred Meyer...254

How You Can Help..255

GLOSSARY..256

Acknowledgements..263

INTRODUCTION

Every two minutes, someone is diagnosed with breast cancer. One in eight women receive this life changing label at some point in their life. It may be you. It may be your mother, your sister, your co-worker, or a friend. But the odds are high that breast cancer has touched your life. No one plans or expects to receive a cancer diagnosis, and yet, we see common threads in the women who fight. We see strength, and bravery. But it isn't just that. We see hope and faith, but it isn't just that either.

The journey through cancer is one that only the travelers themselves can truly explain. It's a journey they never expected to take, and yet, they have been placed in it. They have developed strengths and weaknesses that served them along the way and they have come out the other side different. Very often, they will say they came out better. The struggles and challenges of fighting cancer call out for a level of bravery and strength that most women had yet to face. There is a daily need for honesty and acceptance and determination.

The unintentional sisterhood of breast cancer fighters is forged from the commonality of these qualities and experiences. It is a place where a woman can find comfort and understanding in the absence of pity. It is a place where wounds of the heart can be covered like salve, and hope can be cultivated through shared experiences. This sisterhood is un-covetable and irreplaceable.

Wave After Wave of Pink is a collection of these journeys. May they inspire you, touch you, and guide you on your journey through this life.

Tara L McGuire

Pink Sistas offers women who have been diagnosed with breast cancer no-cost retreats where they find rest and relaxation and meet others who share the same common experiences.
For more information on how you can support this incredible organization, please visit https://pinksistas.org/

Wave after Wave of Pink

Women Warriors Share Tales of the Storm

Every Life Has a Story
Tami Marie Starkey

My name is Tami Marie Starkey. I am forty-four years old and a survivor of stage 2 metastasized breast cancer. My personal journey with cancer started long before I was actually diagnosed. It all began when I was in the third grade and my beloved Aunt Ronda was first diagnosed at the age of thirty-five. I am not sure how much you really know about sickness and disease at that age, but I do remember being deathly afraid of it. To watch my aunt become ill from chemo and radiation and lose her hair and breast really did something to me. She continued to battle cancer for the next six years; unfortunately, she succumbed to the disease at the age of forty-one. Aunt Ronda was not only a teacher, mentor, and inspiration to me, but to hundreds of others as well. Her love and devotion for children was like none other. She would travel up to sixty miles per day from her home in Corbett to where she taught grade school at West Tualatin View Elementary in Portland. If a child was struggling in school, she would encourage them to be the best that they could be. In order to entice her students to strive academically, she would offer a family pet or a weekend retreat to her farm.

As if losing my sweet aunt wasn't enough, history repeated itself with my precious mother Patty. At age fifty-five, her doctor found a lump in her breast during her yearly Papanicolaou. After her diagnosis, I knew it would not be if, but when, I too, would develop breast cancer. She also shared a love and devotion for children. She taught, mentored, and inspired me and hundreds of children at Corbett Grade School. She is strong, supportive, caring, loving, and kind. I am honored and blessed to call her mine! I am ecstatic to announce that my mother is still with us today. She has been cancer free for ten plus years now. Please continue to pray that she will remain healthy and cancer-free for many more years to come.

Because of my family history and having large breasts, I started getting mammograms at thirty. I had dense tissue, which increases your risk of cancer and makes it more difficult to interpret the mammogram. Cancer and dense tissue are both white, which makes it hard to detect the cancer. I was advised that it is like trying to find a polar bear in a blizzard. Those facts were all that I needed; I sent in a request for a prophylactic mastectomy. The doctor couldn't believe that I was willing to go through a major surgery if I didn't have the disease. According to the statistical data, I had only an 18% chance of having cancer. However, he and his data were both wrong. The dye-injected MRI prior to my procedure showed that I did in fact have cancer.

Thinking back and going through my after-visit summaries, I also had warning signs such as dimpling in my skin and an internal itching/burning sensation that I could not scratch. If you have or experienced either of these symptoms, please get to your doctor right away! Early detection is the key to survival. If I can give you one piece of advice, it is this: listen to your body, speak up when something doesn't feel right, and be your own advocate. You are the only one who truly knows how you feel. Get a second opinion if your concerns are overlooked or swept under the rug like mine were. This will not only give you peace of mind but confirmation of the diagnosis.

A good support system is a must! Surround yourself with positive and loving people. It made a huge difference in how I felt, what I thought, and how I acted. I was fortunate to attend the Pink Sistas winter retreat at Government Camp in November 2019. We spent the weekend meditating, making art with trinkets/buttons, and decorating cookies. The retreat not only renewed my heart and soul, it connected me with some amazing, beautiful, and strong women from near and far. Our paths may have never crossed had it not been for Deb Hart and the Pink Sistas retreat.

I would like to personally thank those who have been a major part in my journey. They are the reason that I made it through the darkest days of my life. I am and forever will be thankful for each and every one of you!

The Lord, for dying on the cross so we can have everlasting life, giving me the opportunity to see another day and providing me with the strength and courage to overcome cancer. He has been my rock and foundation in which I can stand firm.

My parents Robert James Jr and Patty Marie Loose, who truly are the World's Greatest! You lead by example—you taught me to be respectful, empathetic, attentive, disciplined, honest, independent, supportive, caring, loving, and kind. Thank you for making me who I am today.

My daughters Hailey Lynn and Hannah Marie Starkey. While you are my biggest fans, supporters, and cheer leaders, you are also my heroes. You have endured so much suffering and loss in your short little lives yet have persevered with dignity and grace. You are loved for the little girls you were, and the special women you have become. I love you the most, my Hailey Bug and Hannah Banana. I thank God for giving me you!

My siblings Jennifer Fowler, Stephanie Paul, and Robert Loose, for being my best friends, reminding me that "we got this," for always having my back, for the many childhood memories and for being the best Aunties and Uncle to my girls.

Nick Clark, for being the handsome cowboy who rode in on a white horse while I was battling a storm within myself during my diagnosis. For showing me chivalry isn't dead: opening doors, calling my father to ask if you could take me out on a date, bringing flowers to my mother and I, and riding at Winchester. If I could go back and change one thing, I would never have pushed you away. It was not fair of me to decide what would be best for you.

Carol Cook, for saving my life not only physically, but mentally as well. You really are my angel on earth! I have greatly enjoyed our time together at church and Bible study, coffee dates, symphonies, berry picking, making cookies, and talking for hours.

Mary Zogg, for giving me peace and comfort, hope and inspiration by showing me that reconstruction surgery can be beautiful. I have greatly enjoyed our time together at church, Bible study, and our walkabouts. Thank you for introducing me to your sweet friend Deb Hart.

Deb Hart, for being the fearless leader and founder of Pink Sistas. Your weekend retreat gave me hope, encouragement and new friendships I will cherish for the rest of my life. You are a life-saver, game changer and an inspiration to so many. I appreciate all you do!

Bruce Ray Evans, for being the dark horse that I never saw coming. You came into my life when I least expected it. For loving me when I didn't want to love myself, giving me a key to your home and to your heart, planting pink flowers, dancing in the living room, singing silly songs while playing the guitar, candle lit dinners, and lots of wine.

While cancer has taken many personal things from me and those that I love most, it also gave me many things to be grateful for. I grew spiritually by drawing closer to God. I learned to give thanks and praise even in the valley. It taught me that each day truly is a gift and to not take it for granted. Thank you for taking the time to read my chapter. May the good Lord bless you and keep you!

Tami Marie Starkey

Tami Marie Starkey is a loving Mother, Daughter, Sister, Aunt and Grandma.

Her two beautiful Daughters are her greatest accomplishments, they are her pride and joy!

She is a native Oregonian who loves Jesus, her family and friends. She is a Christian with morals, values, self-respect and worth. She prays to have eyes that see the best in people, a forgiving heart and a faithful soul. She loves unconditionally, gives without reason and cares for others without expectation.

Despite experiencing many losses throughout her lifetime, she remains thankful for the past, hopeful for the present and optimistic for the future.

Connect with Tami
Facebook: Tami Starkey

WAVE AFTER WAVE OF PINK

Champions Needed

Sherrida Preciado Gates

You are my advocate. Mine and many others who have traveled this path. You bought a copy of this collection of epic stories. You are either a survivor, a supporter, a philanthropist, or curious. Either way, you have lifted our voices with your contribution. I "thank you" for your persistence.

Each of us has a story. It could be sad, scary, frightful, treacherous, happy, ecstatic, or just true to you and me. It is our single line or crack in an individual life. We embody our birth, fears, pain, successes, death, and rebirth. We must incorporate so much into one person and one lifetime and at times, we will need to share our story. I guess that is what I intend to do. For each of you who read this will believe it to be some sort of tribute or a cautionary tale. I hope to leave a mark on you. My intentions are good and fair, not malicious or threatening. For as I speak my history you too could be bound to repeat it to others for their good and so on, as the game of gossip goes.

So many tales and traditions are handed down by women throughout this world. Whether it's at a quilting bee, the wash pool, over the fences, or even at the harvesting fields where they are exchanging their own experiences of pain and suffering. Women carry that burden and this honor. Do these examples sound dated and out of touch? More and more of us are rising up to meet the same challenges as we use Facebook, Twitter, our neighborhood watch, and the schools' and churches' websites accordingly. If we continue to voice our histories out loud and in public, in time it will warrant actions and results. We are all mature and discrete enough to decide what bears repeating. If we remain silent and composed over our endangered health then why would anyone respond and fight for us? All of us have heard this before and we all want it to be true. It starts with this and many hundreds of other stories that will educate our daughters, sisters, aunts, and all the women who will come to pass. This is the 21st century and you would think I was talking of something that happened quite a long time ago when women had very few rights and privileges. We have all heard the time-honored saying "don't wash your dirty laundry in public". This goes beyond that.

Please let me enlighten you on the ever-so-present cause for women and the right to their own choices for their bodily health. Breast cancer was initially a taboo conversation and it was individual activism and support groups that increased its research and education.

While it remained a hidden disease, the funding and advocacy for cancer research and education were little more than what was used to fund an advertisement for toothpaste. With the help of the right people in the right places, the words "breast cancer" and its devastational toll was starting to come into the light. Other women of means and fame, upon dealing with the cavalier attitudes of their doctors who quickly performed mastectomies and never bothered to answer a single question on what other options might be available or what was next for the women post breast cancer, fought for help and education. Our earlier sisters' efforts to develop and fund research, recovery support groups and counseling has been to our advantage. We, today, can benefit from their unselfish actions and we must continue to pay it forward.

Like some women, I knew very little of my moms' side of the family's health history and even less of the other side. I believe what held me together and urged me to work harder for a more positive outcome with my cancer was my intent of giving good history and facts to my daughter. I was not going to allow my children to be swimming in the dark waters that can engulf you during a health crisis, not of their making. I felt way too young for a diagnosis of cancer. I was 45, almost 46. I had a daughter just starting high school and an even younger son. Monica and Jonah are everything to me. I had left my career to raise them and continue to do all I can to be present for their life experiences. At the time of my diagnosis, my husband Craig of 21 years, was moving along in his career, and life was just your basic bliss. We have traveled and lived overseas in Ireland for a few years and were very lucky to visit a lot of countries. We had both been in the military after college and stationed around the states. Our lifestyle choices had been much influenced by this travel and our own decisions to be healthier and fitter than our families. While Craig had a history of growing up without a variety of food options, I was raised by a mother who was a good cook for the times. My moms' family had bouts when each of them was overweight and Craig's family also had some poor eating habits. We ate a little differently and chose to eat locally. I baked our bread and grew a lot of our produce. We were in sports, activities, church, volunteering, and classes, and we had exchange students for many years. We stayed active and healthy in comparison to our familial history. Once I was diagnosed, the research and changes began. I no longer "kick" myself over my apparent decent choices. Maybe too many Guinnesses while living in Ireland or too much sugar visiting other countries? Or maybe I wasn't responsible for my breast cancer. Life is uncertain.

Just missed it

In the early years after our return to the states, we were all connected back to our preferred primary doctors and dentists. I got the kids all their school physicals done and, in the meantime, I was noticing how tired I was. I mentioned it in passing to my primary doctor, he blew it off. I did not take it rudely but just figured he knew best and I was just fine. I guess I just took for granted or maybe burdened him to be able to look at me and know all there is to know, medically speaking that is. For the next 2-3 years, I made a number of appointments looking for an answer to why I was always tired. It was never even a blip on the radar of what might be going on.

In the years leading up to my diagnosis, I lost a brother to suicide, another brother and his family were having devastating difficulties and the job security at my husband's company was shaky. Isn't there something about the trouble that comes in "3"?

My doctor gave me a plethora of choices for my state of health. I was told how I was aging, had a busy life with very active children and I could expect to see a little drop in my energy once in a while. These answers were fine for a portion of the time. Now, I look at everything through different lenses. I truly didn't have many health issues and never needed to be worried or ask for more. Didn't even think I had the right to ask for anything. The adage about the "customer always being right" never seems to fit in the medical office. No one ever asked for blood work or had me on anything other than patronizing responses. I started to get frustrated. I was not sleeping well, gaining weight, depressed, and not in pain, but had some anxiety. Apparently, you can feel this way and your doctor will bless you with how well you are coping with motherhood.

I had my first mammogram at 45, almost 46. There was nothing they saw out of the ordinary. Good. I didn't expect anything irregular. I was scheduled to get my son in for some shots before school started at our primary care facility.

All was going well; they were late but that was usually the case these days. I needed to know how much longer, as he and I were getting cranky. When we finally got in, after the shots, my doctor asked my son to wait outside the door while he spoke to me. He let me know he had just been placed in charge of the facility and wanted to know how I felt about the service. I felt a little rewarded because he wanted my opinion. Lucky me. I was honest but curtailed. "Well, it was fine. I felt it had gotten a little harder to make appointments and get seen on time recently." He thanked me and then promptly let me know I needed to find a better-suited facility as I seemed rather frustrated at times with him. I had been "fired".

I literally broke down and cried. In hindsight, he had not been able to find what was wrong with me, so "I" was the problem. I had continued to express doubt about his diagnosis therefore "I" needed to leave. I was awestruck. It's hard to find primary care doctors in the area and I was being cast out without a net of hope to get me back in. It was like a bad breakup. Do you know what they say about those types of relationships? Incredible changes are about to happen. Now I needed to take better control of what I had power over.

Shake myself awake

Over the past 12 years and plenty during my treatment years, I questioned and researched how to "not do" or "not eat" or "not think". I truly believe information seeking was my coping measure. In gathering the most up-to-date information, I can regain control and understand my situation and deal with the topics that arise.

I have volunteered with support programs that have: put on education seminars, been a speaker myself, conferences, runs, walks, fashion shows, fly fishing, auctions, intimacy courses, cooking classes, make-up aid, massages, journaling, yoga, dieticians, and partook in all that assisted cancer survivors.

I found my family was learning from me and my experience. My own friends and community started to ask me for information or at least direction.

Early on, my parents and in-laws could not see the treatment or the support as anything more than prolonging the inevitable. I believe they became a little more enlightened with our choices. My journey was quite arduous and very scary. After being set adrift by my longtime primary care group, I just paused for a bit. Other things were going on and I was getting back into the work field, it just was too much to handle for the times. The rest of the family was still welcome at the clinic, just not me. I made an appointment with my gynecologist for the annual. I told her how I felt and asked her about the weight gain, under the arm. At first, I got the same little "oh, you're getting older and hormones are changing to create fatty areas around your body". Now, I am petite, 5"2' and I have stayed pretty much in shape. I was in the military and knew I had to keep taking care of myself and was determined to do so. I asked her about scheduling some way to look into the area better. It wasn't symmetrical. After it came back, we noted an "area of concern", then we got the ball rolling. It was diagnosed as triple positive (ER, HER2, and PR) Ductal carcinoma in situ (dcis), stage IIB. The HER2 protein positivity was attracting the most attention from medical professionals. The tumor was quite large and it was aggressive. After surgery had established the cancer had not spread to my lymphatic system, I was navigated towards my treatment plan. As we do not live anywhere near either of our families, my best friend and husband set up fantastic support from everywhere. Church, work, and community all came in on the proverbial white horses, granting my every spoken need and the unspoken wishes.

Adorn my cape

As the signs of my adapting to the breast cancer diagnosis started to appear Craig was working to provide the practical support, which helped in maintaining my self-confidence. He is after all a chemical engineer. The depression and anxiety that often set in were clear signs I did not feel in control. My life had drastically changed. This to your basic cancer "muggles" seems somewhat obvious but for those in the trenches, it was HELL and I feared never returning to who I had worked so hard to become. A PTSD sense for the loss and unconsciousness to all, that was me. I was going through three years plus of aggressive chemotherapy, radiation therapy, infusions for HER2+, more surgery, and aromatase inhibitors. My side effects were all over the map. I was thrown cruelly into post-menopause and am still receiving those gifts. Even today, I still have uncomfortable CIPN (chemo-induced peripheral neuropathy,) osteopenia, continued cognitive challenges, and your run of the mill intimacy struggles. My journey was similar in many ways to others around me, but I really would not have been aware of them without the support of many programs delivered unselfishly. You see those who advocated for changes, empowerment, and no more silence about breast cancer are the true heroes. They were there to ask: How does one deal with the guilt of putting your children through this? Navigate the negative tendencies into positive thinking. The managing of distress, balancing work and cancer, and simply not wallowing in self-hate and pity. The feelings of complete and utter inadequacy in your relationship. "My body, my goodness what is happening?" These were all a part of the forever journey I continue.

The programs that are worth your money, energy, and promotion, are the ones in which cancer survivors bare their souls or not. Retreats like the ones put on by Pink Sistas in Portland, Oregon. They allow you to come, in peace, to accept yourself for where you are and be loved by a sisterhood that you now belong to. It is how one moves on. Moving on is not a direction per se, more of an acknowledgment. Most Cancer survivors like to know where they are at, where they have been and a little insight into where they might be headed. One must advocate for themselves by choosing a direction. An informed and supported path and speaking up about it never hurts either.

You know I just wanted to follow up on the primary care doctor who fired me. I'd like to say he sent me cards and flowers, reporting he had changed his ways and was truly sorry, but you know better. What did occur was; that while out having coffee with a friend I bumped into him. I said hello and asked if he remembered me, it had been 4 years. He replied yes and asked how I was doing. I exclaimed how he had saved my life. I graciously thanked him for his due diligence in kicking me out of his practice 4 years ago. I went on to explain, yes calmly, I had survived breast cancer and had he not pushed me to look elsewhere for a better, more thorough physician, I might not be standing here in front of him today. He had a wide-eyed look of "oh crap". I said in a very kind and professional voice, "maybe in the future, when a female patient is telling you she is not feeling well and her body, which she has lived in for a long time and knows well, is telling her something is wrong. You might listen and take her for her word and try harder." He gave a slight smile of acknowledgment and we said our goodbyes.

I put the task in front of you all. Maybe most important, is to never give up on getting an answer that allows peace, because most of us know when something isn't right.

Sherrida Preciado Gates

Sherri Gates grew up in a military family and moved often as a young girl. She comes from a large family, easily made friends, and quickly got involved wherever they were stationed.

She joined the United States Air force after graduating college and several years doing social work. She loved the military and the educational opportunities available for her to pursue. Sherri and her husband Craig met while both were serving in the military.

Sherri and Craig have two children, Monica and Jonah. The family lived in Ireland for two years and they love to travel. The children were experts at packing and pulling their bags everywhere they visited.

Craig accepted a job in the Pacific Northwest after graduation, so Sherri finished her military obligation and they moved west.

Sherri loves her home, and although she can make a home anywhere, she is happy to stay where she is.

"Adventure always awaits!"

Connect with Sherri
Email: svgates8@gmail.com
Facebook: Sherri Gates

WAVE AFTER WAVE OF PINK

Gifts and Silver Linings
Jennie Vinson

My name is Jennie, and in 2014, just 6 days after my 37th birthday, I was diagnosed with Stage 2B Triple Positive Breast Cancer. To say this was a shock would be a complete understatement. I had an almost 3-year-old son, had just begun a new dream job at a great company, and clearly had no time for chemotherapy in my life.

Since I was so young, I had never had a mammogram. Looking back, this was most likely a mistake, as my grandmother had been diagnosed with her first breast cancer at the age of 41. At that time, there was no such thing as chemotherapy or radiation, so her chances of survival were dim. Her biggest fear was that she wouldn't live to be at my father's Bar Mitzvah, just 2 years away. That's the fear that all mothers face when they receive a cancer diagnosis. The fear that they won't be able to mother their child.

They threw the treatment book at me, starting just 10 days after my diagnosis– I did 6 rounds of chemo over 18 weeks, a double mastectomy and then 35 radiation sessions. I decided to do reconstruction with implants so I have had two additional surgeries as well. It was definitely a marathon, not a sprint and I was very fortunate to have an amazing team of family and friends who supported me all the way through the process.

One thing that I was able to do that I really believed help me get through all of the ups and downs of treatment was to work with a naturopath who specialized in cancer treatment. He and my oncologist collaborated on my treatment plan so that I was able to use some secondary treatments to offset some of the many side effects that I experienced. I took a ridiculous number of supplements each day, fasted in the days leading up to my chemo treatment and did Vitamin C infusions. I also did regular acupuncture and physical therapy appointments. All of these things were invaluable in supporting my quality of life, allowing me to continue to work and travel throughout most of the experience.

The other thing that I did that I believe really helped me get through my treatment, was to work with a fitness trainer who focused on working exclusively with cancer patients. It felt so empowering to be lifting weights and to be moving my body. It helped me to feel alive at a time when the treatments were taking so much from me. It was amazing that I was able to increase my weight threshold throughout treatment and it was also really great to be working out with other cancer patients.

Even with all of this support, at times during my cancer treatment, fear would grip me. And to be honest, sometimes it still does even 6 years later. But now, instead of dwelling on the what-ifs, I've chosen to focus on the gifts and the silver linings that my cancer diagnosis and treatment has provided me.

From the very beginning, I knew that my cancer diagnosis had to be about something more significant. It gave me great comfort to think of my breast cancer as a teacher, a teacher that I would ask to leave my body, but a teacher nonetheless.

I'm going to share some silver linings and gifts I've received with the hope that by sharing them with you that maybe you'll add these gifts to your list as you or your loved one navigates this journey.

One of my greatest gifts has been the shift to not taking any time with family, expressly my husband and son, for granted. They are my heaven on earth. I also have the best relationship with my siblings and my parents that I've ever had. There is a level of transparency and honesty that I wouldn't trade for the world, a knowing that the little things aren't that big of a deal. The little annoyances of life are still there, like when the toilet seat gets left up in the middle of the night, but cancer gave me the gift of perspective. And so now I only stay mad at my husband Scott for 2 minutes instead of 10 when sitting down on the seatless toilet. It's about progress, not perfection. Am I right?

Another gift that cancer has given is the ability to live firmly in the here and now and make the most out of every moment. Now it would be a bit of a cliche to say that I can do this 24/7. But I find it much simpler to do this now that I'm a cancer survivor. A few years back, my son Oscar, who is now nine years old, suggested we eat candy for breakfast. My initial instinct as a "proper" mother was, of course, to say no, but then I thought, "what would it hurt?". Soon we were sprinkling jelly beans on our oatmeal and giggling at what a treat we were sharing. His smile and his disbelief at the wonder of getting to eat candy for breakfast is something that I'll never forget. He probably won't either! And you know what? He ate more of that oatmeal than he had ever eaten before. I call that a mom win for sure.

My breast cancer diagnosis has gifted me with the ability to lighten up about most everything and to laugh at things that would have had me crying before my diagnosis. After my first surgery, a double mastectomy, three-year-old Oscar asked me if he could see my "owies". Terror gripped me as I contemplated the fear that I would inflict on his little heart when he saw the two large scars across my chest. While I was going through my treatment, my biggest worry was how this was going to impact him. But not wanting to create fear of the unknown, I slowly pulled down my tank top and showed him my chest. With wide eyes and in all earnestness, he looked at me and said, "Mama did a ninja do that to you?"

With a huge sigh of relief and a wide grin on my face, I said, "Yes! Her name is Ninja Naik, some people call her doctor, but we know who she really is!"

So now, my most splendid silver lining is that my son thinks that I did battle with a ninja and that I won! With just a few battle scars to show for it.

One of the most cathartic silver linings about my breast cancer experience has been the certainty and comfort that I have in knowing how profoundly loved I am by my family and community. Chemo and cancer changed who I am by deepening the level of intention and integrity in my life, creating discipline about what matters most, and has shone a light on my ability to persevere. My time on this grand planet is precious, and I want to make the most of every minute. So, I've said goodbye to laziness, goodbye to complacency, and see you later to excuses. Cancer has helped me welcome a whole new level of commitment, passion, focus, perception, consciousness, and compassion for myself, my family, and my community.

Since my diagnosis in 2014, I have been fortunate to attend several retreats for young breast cancer survivors. This has included learning how to surf in Maui, riding the whitewater of the Snake River and of course the wonderful Pink Sistas retreat at the floating home on the Columbia River. Each one of these experiences has given me the ability to reflect on how far I've come and to surround myself with people who "get it" and who allow me to be right where I'm at with my feelings and my experience.

These retreats have provided me a great deal of healing, because it's not just the physical wounds that must be tended to during your cancer treatment. The emotional and spiritual wounds that the chemo can't fix have remained long after the cancer left my body. Meeting and spending time with other cancer survivors helped me to navigate this "new normal". I'm excited to say that I've met some of my best girlfriends at these retreats as a result of having had cancer. What's so nice is that as the years go by, our conversations are no longer dominated by what types of implants we have or what our treatment schedules are. Now we are able talk about our families and our gardens and our hopes and our dreams. We do all of this with a deep knowing of the gratitude we share for the lives we get to lead.

The gifts of cancer that have been given have been profound and are uncovered to me daily. These gifts facilitate more precious attention to the things that matter to me most and are something that, while I wish I hadn't had to have cancer to receive, I would never want to give back.

And back to my grandmother. She did live to see my father at his bar mitzvah. She lived to see me get married and to meet my baby son. She lived until she was 93. My hope is that my greatest gift will be that she and I will also share the longevity gene that she seemed to have and ultimately, the opportunity to live the long full life that she did.

Jennie Vinson was diagnosed with Stage 2B Triple positive breast cancer in 2014 when she was 37 years old. She is a mom, a wife, a marketing consultant, and a yoga instructor. She lives with her husband Scott, 9-year-old son Oscar and her dad on a small farm in rural Oregon. She enjoys cooking delicious meals, growing beautiful flowers in her garden, and looking for ways to make the world a more equitable, just place.

Connect with Jennie:
Email: jennie@jennievinson.com
Facebook: Jennie Breslow Vinson
Instagram: @stillfiremovement or @jennieloulou
Website: www.stillfiremovement.com

WAVE AFTER WAVE OF PINK

My Marathon
Leslie Kerwin Myll

My name is Leslie and I am a 59-year-old woman who was diagnosed in September 2018 with Invasive Lobular Carcinoma, ILC. My husband and I had recently moved to Bend, Oregon. One night while turning over in bed I felt an unusual sensation in my right breast. It was not a palpable mass, instead, the area felt very thick. I phoned my Dr. in CA and she placed an order for both a 3D mammogram and an ultrasound.

I have always been diligent about staying on top of my appointments. Because of my dense breast and calcium deposits, I was being monitored every 6 months. I told myself it was likely nothing serious. I had a 3D mamo which did not show anything suspicious. Next stop, ultrasound. I told the technician to press hard and that it would not hurt me. She proceeded and seemed to find something. I heard the click, click from the keyboard as she was tying away. We, women, know that means something is there. She left the room to talk with the radiologist. Minutes felt like hours. The radiologist came in and sat down beside me. He let me know that there was an area that needed to be biopsied. It wasn't my first biopsy so I tried hard not to worry. I know, easier said than done. I had the biopsy a couple of days later and the Dr. asked if they had the results back by Friday would I be willing to hear the results over the phone. I agreed.

The dreaded phone call came and the doctor asked if it was a convenient time to talk. My heart sank. I said yes but that I wanted to get my husband. We heard the word cancer together. The air was quickly being sucked out of the room as I fell into my husband's arms. We gathered ourselves and then let him know that we had just moved to town and I didn't even have a primary doctor yet. We asked him who he would recommend and he gave us the name of his mother-in-law's surgeon. If it was good enough for her it was good enough for me. As it would turn out it was a great referral. Their office coordinated everything and I would meet with my surgeon Monday morning. I remember going to bed that evening and feeling numb. I would softly cry and my husband would hold me tight and whisper in my ear "We got this". It was in the middle of that very dark night I began to journal.

My first entry:

My Marathon

This all-weekend felt like a big, blurry fog. One minute you are doing something routine and the next you are pulled into a new reality that you don't even recognize. You hear the statistics and see the pink ribbons. Your heart aches for those women and their families but you don't see yourself hearing that news that unexpectedly makes you part of that "club".

I cry softly while my mind races past NOW. The "what if's". So much is flooding in that I realize I am hearing only part of it. I have the great fortune to have my beloved Don. He catches what I drop. He is my brave warrior who always provides safety. This, though, he cannot fix. He cannot heal me. He will stand beside me and help me gain strength. He will encourage me to scream and shout BLEEP CANCER. We took a walk in the forest today and I did scream. I knew that release was necessary. He celebrated my outburst. There will be many more to come. I am keenly aware that this is now my marathon.

The weekend seemed so long and here we sat, across from my surgeon. She calmly explained the potential scenarios. An MRI was ordered for the next day. We learned that a lumpectomy would not be an option. The only card on the table was a Mastectomy. Now the decisions would have to be made rather quickly. Did I want to spare my nipple? What a thing to contemplate. My left breast looked clean on all scans yet some women take the other breast as a precaution. That night we discussed it in depth. My husband was fighting back the tears and I realized this was also a loss for him. The breast is a very sensual part of a woman's anatomy. We had always shared a very close intimacy. How would this change us? We both cried and came to the conclusion I would have a bilateral mastectomy, nipples and all.

My Plastic Surgeon was in the operating room during the surgery. Expanders were put in under the muscle in my chest. Yes, it's painful. Over time this helps stretch the skin which is necessary if I wanted to have reconstruction down the line. When I woke from the surgery, I learned that the cancer had spread to my lymph nodes and more were being tested. I was scared. Pathology came back cancer present in 4 of the 9 lymph nodes. I knew that meant aggressive treatment was in store. Both Chemo and Radiation would be needed. The decision to take the left breast was the correct one as they found a different breast cancer in that breast. It was Ductal Carcinoma In-Situ, too small to be seen on imaging. I was so thankful I listened to that inner voice and thanked my Guardian Angel.

My Second Journal Entry:

Evil Cells

You are not welcome in my home

You are not invited and cannot dwell here!

Though you try to wreak havoc, I will fight you with everything I've got.

You may be here temporarily but do not get too comfortable as I assure you,

I will take this on as a mission. To wipe out your cruel intention.

AND I will NEVER, EVER give you power over me.

Chemo would soon follow. The thought of my long hair coming out in big chunks terrified me. I decided that I would have my head shaved. There had to be something I could control. My husband photographed. My hairdresser first put my hair in a ponytail. I did not face the mirror. She then began shaving my head. He captured moments of both bravery and heartache.

I wanted to be brave and strong. Be a good sport. Frequently people just don't know what to say. Others try and express their optimism that you might not be prepared to hear. I was having the single most sensual part of my femininity being amputated along with knowing there is cancer inside of me. The very last thing I wanted to hear was "Everything will be ok". NOOO. Everything was not ok. I had those days when pushing through the chemo was all I could muster. It was in the quiet moments that I would permit myself to be sad while trying to be mindful that this is not a place to stay and stew for too long. I have been blessed with a loving family, amazing friends, and great co-workers and they all rallied around me.

My best friend heard the news over text. I was on the phone with the Dr. when I texted her. She was waiting for the results and I knew she was eager to know. I simply put "Buy Head Scarves." She knew what that meant. We would talk and cry later that night. I told her "For heaven's sake, we just got here and now I am BOOBLESS in Bend. Well, she took that on as her mission and had 200 Pink bracelets made with "BOOBLESS in Bend, Leslie Kerwin Myll. 2018." Pretty soon there were friends, family, and coworkers all over the country with bracelets she had mailed out. I would get pictures from my construction team on tractors wearing the bracelets, babies, fence posts, and family across America. It really was amazing.

When the "C" word hits you, it really knocks you off your feet. There is such a structure to treatment it resembled a job. Chemotherapy was for three months. Reconstruction would follow and then 25 rounds of radiation. I feel blessed to have had such wonderful care. I felt connected to these people who dedicate their entire lives to helping others preserve theirs.

The night before my last round of Radiation I penciled this entry.

255 Days

To my Body that carried me these last 255 days...I say Thank You

To my Head that had to work so hard to keep my wits when it all seemed too overwhelming...I say Thank You

To my Heart for allowing me to feel the pain, the fear, the loss, the sadness, and the truth... I say Thank You.

To my Pride, for letting go of you which allowed me to accept help from others...I say Thank You.

To my Eyes for allowing me to witness so many "God Moments".... I say Thank You

To my Spirit, though beaten and battered, never broke...I say Thank You

For the gift of my Faith that flows through me...I could not imagine this walk without you, Lord...I say Thank You

The victory is not in winning the race but in finishing it. Breast cancer does not only change your body, it also changes you.

There have been so many times I have said I was going to slow down. I was so caught up in moving forward. Part of that grind we can so easily get caught up in. I recognize that moving forward is of no value if you don't look up and take the time to see what is around you. There have been so many blessings with so many kind and special people. Strangers lifted my spirits. My doctors, nurses, PT, chemo and radiation techs, integrative therapy, my treasured family and friends who have all loved me through this...
I say Thank You.

I was introduced to a group of women who had or were going through cancer. My physical therapist was wonderful and encouraged me to give it a try. I did and immediately was happy I followed her advice. It is in the series of connections that fate finds meaning. Through this group, I made a new contact with the Pink Sistas.

Pink Sista's is an organization run by a tireless soldier, Deb Hart. She has devoted her life to helping women with breast cancer in Oregon. Being a thriver, herself, she knows all too well the feeling of being overwhelmed by the diagnosis. I was introduced to her by another thriver and invited to be a guest on her floating home on the Columbia River. It was to be a weekend of fella Sista's being pampered by her. She would make the meals, take us out on the boat, and arrange yoga and jewelry classes. It sounded too good to be true. I jumped at the chance and said YES. Later I started getting cold feet. I didn't know any of these women and had only talked to Deb over the phone. I was chickening out but knew I had to push myself outside of my comfort level. I arranged to go with another lady from Bend and we would share that 3-hour drive together. By the time we got there, I had met a new friend. It was a remarkable weekend. Six of us plus Deb would share our stories, laugh and cry together. Encourage and listen. Some would open up and cry that they had not known how to talk about it. Just sharing with other women who truly know is so comforting. We all said our goodbyes that Sunday afternoon, all of us promising to keep in touch. The night I got home I reflected on the weekend and how powerful it was. We need each other in a way that our friends and family can't accommodate.

Journal Entry:

Stairs

We all took the same path up those stairs. Most of us, are apprehensive. What awaits? The reality is that anytime you bring strangers together it is a bit intimidating. What does this weekend even look like? None of us knew and what unfolded was purely organic. You cannot script this journey...It must be felt and lived to be appreciated...This weekend represented putting down my warrior armor and allowing myself to be vulnerable. To be with women who understand...It has truly been an honor to be part of this experience, one that will continue to grow. Deb has given us a much bigger gift than this incredible weekend...She has given us a shared bond...I will forever be grateful I took those steps up those stairs and met all of you beautiful, strong, kind, and inspiring women.

This journey has been filled with so many emotions. My perspective has certainly changed. Time becomes more precious and how I chose to spend it, is more meaningful. I have had some setbacks physically as a result of radiation. It is very important before they decide to have reconstruction. Radiation can have some serious side effects. Most women will do alright but radiating stretched skin has its challenges. Ultimately, I ended up with a capsular contraction. My grapefruit breast was turning into a lemon. It was so tight it looked like it would pop. My plastic surgeon urged me to have surgery to remove the implant and he would replace it with a smaller one. BAD IDEA. If my skin was that transparent then another implant didn't stand a chance. Since I had severe fibrosis, I was not a candidate for this. I know now I should have been consulting with my radiation oncologist. There seems to be a disconnect between Plastic Surgeons and Oncology. I was unaware that the multiple surgeries would create more fibrosis. The surgeon knew this but did the replacement implant. Five weeks later my chest opens up in the middle of the night as my skin was too thin to support that implant. I was rushed to the emergency room. I lost my breast, again.

I hope I can share what I have learned along the way. It is important women understand the potential outcomes that might occur. It is also important that the team of doctors, work in concert with one another. I had an amazing oncologist, general surgeon as well as radiation oncologist. The bridge between the plastic surgeon was not in place and so I trusted blindly his recommendation. I hope to bring awareness to anyone who is undergoing treatment to check in with their entire team to make sure the recommendations are sound.

I am incredibly grateful that I am currently in remission and thank God every day that I am alive.

Leslie Kerwin Myll

Leslie Kerwin Myll was diagnosed with breast cancer in the Fall of 2018. Born and raised in Southern California she earned her BS from Chapman University and began her career with a Fortune 100 company. Her love of design and real estate pulled her in a new direction where she established a long career in real estate with a builder/developer.

While traveling with her husband to Bend, Oregon they realized this was a place they wanted to call home. With their children grown, they took a leap and made the move. Within weeks of moving, she was diagnosed with invasive lobular carcinoma. "What, there is more than one kind of Breast Cancer?" She quickly learned that ILC requires a different screening protocol and ultrasound is necessary for women with fibrocystic and dense breast. She is an advocate for educating women about this important information because too often it is found at a more advanced stage. She is a licensed OR Broker and is excited about her new future.

Connect with Leslie:
Email: Leslie@fredrealestate.com
Cell: 541-604-0197
Interiors by Leslie
Email: Gustologan@gmail.com
Cell: 541-699-2636

WAVE AFTER WAVE OF PINK

Roll of the Dice

Kortnee Colbry

In February 2016, in the evening after getting my kids to bed, I kissed my husband good night and lay in bed to unwind and watch a reality show. I had an itch near my left breast in my underarm. I felt a little lump, and I thought, "That's weird." It was a pea-sized, hard, ball. I felt the other breast; it wasn't there. I asked my husband to feel it, and he said maybe it was just from breastfeeding, but it had been months since I stopped. I'll go to the doctor for anything. As I always tell my husband, "Safety is sexy!"

I made an appointment with my wonderful primary care doctor, Dr. Wu. She said I was pretty young—I was thirty-five at the time—had no family history and was in good health; it was probably nothing, but she would be happy to run a mammogram for me. I agreed; I needed a mammogram just to ease my mind. It was scheduled for a week later. The machine needed repairs, so another week. I went in with my husband and the young ultrasound tech said, you can see the region right there, there's something; I'll have the radiologist look. Then I was told I needed a biopsy the next day. I was nervous going in. My husband went with me, but I thought no way did I have cancer. After all, my primary care doctor told me I was too young, and I had no family history. I thought it was probably just benign.

On the day of my biopsy, I remember chatting with the medical assistant. As we had kids around the same age, the radiologist didn't even look at me. She kept a great poker face. I remember asking how long it would take until I get the results, and I was told a few days. That was the longest week ever! I called on Friday and they said the results weren't in yet. I had to wait through the weekend. I remember my husband driving me to this park that overlooks Portland, and I said to him, "I think I have breast cancer." He said we didn't have the results yet. I told him everything is going too well in life: my salon is taking off, you are a wonderful husband, the kids are happy... but I have a feeling it's cancer. We drove home and I prayed all night.

The next day, a Monday, I took my son to preschool, then came home and put my daughter in her high chair while I was making her breakfast. The phone rang, it was the radiologist. She said, "I have your results, and I'm sorry to tell you this, but you have breast cancer." I was shaking. She said, "Get a pen because I need you to write down some information." She told me it was Stage 1, estrogen positive, HER2 negative. (Whatever that means, I thought.) I was told I would need to meet with the surgeon and an oncologist.

I did not want to call my husband; he is a teacher and I didn't want to disrupt his class. I called my mom crying, she just said, "I love you, honey; I'll talk to you later" and hung up the phone. Which is not like my mom. Next, I called my sister. Luckily, she was on her break at work. I told her they called, and I had breast cancer. She said, "You're going to kick this breast cancer! We're going to get you cool hats and scarves and big earrings. Don't even worry, I'm here for you." I'm more of a stressed person and my sister doesn't worry much; she's the calm to my crazy. A few minutes later my cousin and then my brother walked through the door. My mom had called them, and they came right over. Family is everything to me, and they all are amazing!

My mom sent me a text saying she was picking my son up from preschool and coming over. The preschool teacher was one of my best friends. When she saw my mom pick up my son instead of me, she said, "Oh, Kortnee has cancer, doesn't she?" I'll always remember that the next day she gave me a box of sunshine; everything in it was yellow. It's the little things like that that I remember.

My mom told me I should call my husband, and I wish I hadn't. I said, "I'm okay, but it's cancer. Don't come home, we'll chat after work." He said he held it together at work, then lost it on his way home. He walked through the door and we cried together and hugged. We started researching everything we could right away.

That evening my sister, my sister-in-law, and my aunts all came over and brought food. I couldn't eat, I kept hyperventilating and crying. Trying to go to sleep that night, I kept waking up, thinking it was a nightmare. I couldn't control my tears. My husband would wake up and just hold me. When you hear the word cancer, I thought it meant you were dying. I have a one-year-old and a three-year-old; this can't happen to me.

I had my first appointment at the amazing Compass Oncology at Providence Portland. My first oncologist was a tough personality, someone you want for oncology. I'm not sure we would ever be friends, but I wanted her as my doctor. She was great, as was the oncology surgeon, also at Providence Portland. They were both amazing. I had to answer a lot of questions about family history, have blood tests, scans, etc. I also had to decide if I wanted a double mastectomy or a lumpectomy. I thought of Giuliana Rancic. I used to watch her reality show. She had a double mastectomy and the show followed her journey. Then I remembered my brother-in-law's ex-girlfriend had breast cancer when she was in her twenties. I reached out to her on Facebook. She had a lumpectomy. She said, "If I had to do it all again, I would've had a double mastectomy first," because her cancer came back. She said that the only reason she had chosen not to was that she was a single mom of two boys at the time. She said, "Kortnee if you have the help, get a mastectomy." I did more research and saw more doctors for second opinions. I scheduled a double mastectomy for three weeks later. My husband told me it was my decision and he would support my choice.

I met with the plastic surgeon who would put tissue expanders in right after the double mastectomy. The morning of my surgery, we parked at Providence Portland. There is a cross is at the top of the hospital, and a Catholic chapel inside. I went to the chapel that morning, crying and praying were all I could do.

I had a full room of guests: my husband, my sister, my brother, sister-in-law, my mom, my dad, and my two aunts. They were all there for me.

After a long surgery, the doctors told my husband and parents they had removed the cancer and it had not spread to the lymph nodes. Hallelujah! I remember being very sore and out of it, but seeing my family staying there all day made me feel loved.

I was in the hospital for a few days and then returned home with drain tubes. My husband was the best nurse, he changed drain tubes and managed my meds. My wonderful mother-in-law "Mima" took over my mommy duties. My daughter was just one year old. She would be in her crib and I would hear her cry at night. I would walk into her room, but I couldn't pick her up. It broke my heart. Thankfully, my mother-in-law moved in with us and would meet me in my baby girl's room and pick her up and rock her for me. I still thank her every day for all she does. I was part of a Mom's Club and they had set up a meal train for us. Food was delivered to our home every night for thirty days; it was amazing and helped us out so much.

After recovery, I had to go in and get my tissue expanders slowly pumped up. My sister told me she thought it looked like a balloon blowing up when she took me. It stretched the muscles and was super painful. I always joked I don't know how Dolly Parton did it!

My oncologist called me and said my Oncotype score was at 11%, meaning low cancer recurring. She wanted me to start chemo in April. I had twelve rounds, once every other week for six months. I was able to have the low-dose chemo. I was happy I didn't lose my hair; however, I had a lot of side effects and definitely did not feel well. I was able to keep working in my salon. I was also exercising.

My yoga instructor was diagnosed with the same type of breast cancer as I was just one month before my diagnosis. I reached out to her, we went through our journey together, and are now great friends. I have learned so much about health, fitness, and nutrition from her. Eating healthy and doing normal activities with my kids, husband, and family. I feel blessed.

My wonderful friend Alisiha took me to my chemo appointments, and she lived almost an hour away. She kept me laughing, which really is the best medicine.

Once chemo was over, I wanted to have the expanders changed out for implants as soon as possible because I had booked a trip to Mexico before I was diagnosed. I really wanted saline implants because I'm more of a natural person, but my doctor talked me out of it and said the gummy bear silicone implants look best in reconstruction patients. I went with the doctor's recommendation.

The surgery went as expected. I was sent home with drain tubes. Unfortunately, I was chasing after my one-year-old, and I kind of tripped—and she accidentally pulled the drain tube out. I caught a breast infection and was in the hospital for five days. The Infectious Disease Control team came in every day. Luckily, they were able to drain it and the antibiotics worked. I missed my Mexico vacation, but being healthy and not needing another surgery was most important.

My doctor told me I should start Tamoxifen; it stops estrogen production in your body. The type of breast cancer I have is *"the kind to get"* because they know how to treat it: stop all estrogen. I didn't want to take the Tamoxifen because I had read all the side effects: taking it long-term is not good for you. I recalled reading Giuliana Rancic's book, and at the end of her book she noted that she looks at the pill before she takes it; she knows this pill is going to do her body good and keep her healthy, and it's worth the side effects. I think that every night as I still take Tamoxifen.

Giuliana Rancic has a breast cancer foundation called Fab-U-Wish. I wrote to her foundation and told her how her book and TV show helped me through my breast cancer journey. My wish was to meet her. I got the next best thing, a phone call from her on June 2. We were able to chat about cancer, kids, life, and health. Best. Gift. Ever. I admire her and look up to her so much!

My oncologists suggested that since I'd had two children, I should likely get a hysterectomy. I was doing monthly shots in my tummy to put me in menopause and stop my estrogen. I had three doctors' opinions, and they all recommended it since my cancer was estrogen-positive.

In November 2017, I had the hysterectomy. The surgery went as expected, and recovery was not as bad as the other surgeries. It was difficult in my mid-thirties to be in my first year of going into menopause; I didn't feel normal, and it was so hard physically and emotionally. This is another chapter to write on, next time!

Pink Sistas

My retreat weekend will always hold a special place in my heart. Deb is so welcoming; from the moment you walk in the door. She made me feel so comfortable and the retreat weekend took my mind off of my life issues and allowed me to relax. There was paddle boarding, yoga, amazing food, and conversation with the other women on the retreat. I tell so many people about Pink Sistas retreats. It was nice to share my story and listen to the stories of other women who are going through it all, too.

Whenever I have fear or anxiety (which is often) I still think of the conversations I have had with Deb. Not only during my retreat weekend but also in phone calls and messages. If I could give a humanitarian award, it would be awarded to Deb Hart for all she has done – not only for me but for other breast cancer survivors and thrivers.

Toxic Implants

In 2019, I began feeling ill, right before the Pink Sistas retreat. I thought it may have been due to the side effects of chemo, Tamoxifen, or menopause. I had a checkup with my plastic surgeon and found out the silicone implants were on a recall. Some were leaking and causing cancer of the immune system. Luckily mine were not leaking, but I was having weird symptoms. I was seeing my naturopathic doctor and medical doctor, and every test was coming back normal. But I was lightheaded, I had vision issues, nerve issues, and I was so weak and tired.

I decided I wanted these toxic implants taken out. I had the implants removed in November 2019 and replaced them with saline implants. Dr. Bartholomew did a wonderful job swapping implants. The saline implants look and feel more comfortable and natural than the silicone ones had. I'm feeling better now in February 2020.

I have learned so much about health, hormones, cancer, supplements vitamins, exercise, and food. It has been life-changing for me. I still ask every Eastern and Western doctor I see, "Why do you think I got breast cancer?" I was told one in eight women get breast cancer. Line up eight friends, roll the dice, and one of you will get it. Your age and family history don't matter, one in eight will get it.

I'm doing everything I can to keep myself healthy and stress-free. I would like to share everything I know now and what I've been through, so please feel free to contact me.

Thank You

Thank you to Compass Oncology; A Woman's Time—Dr. Tori Hudson, Dr. Rebecca Reese, Dr. Wu, Dr. Imatani, Dr. Bartholomew, Dr. Finch, Dr. Krien, and Dr. Drake.

Deb Hart and Pink Sistas, and Dr. Solti, the sweetest oncologist. My physical therapists. All my family and friends. My mother-in-law, Mima. My son and daughter, who always remind me to slow down and Namaste. They ask, "Is this healthy to eat?" And they wake me up to start yoga every morning.

And my biggest cheerleading doctor, nurse, teacher, researcher, comedian, and loving husband . . . I love you!

Peace, love, health, and happiness to you all!

Kortnee Colbry is an esthetician and the owner of Eyeland Beauty.

She graduated from Boise State University and is a devoted Bronco fan.

Kortnee has an amazing husband and two awesome kids, a seven-year-old son, and a five-year-old daughter. She loves Yoga and the Hawaiian Islands.

She is passionate about researching health and nutrition.

Connect with Kortnee:
Instagram: @eyelandbeautykortnee
Website: www.eyelandbeauty.com

My Story

Lisa Warzyn

Hello, my name is Lisa Warzyn. I was diagnosed with lobular breast cancer at age 47. I was dating but single with no children. To date, I've had 17 surgeries/biopsies to my chest and 2 sets of implants. Before all this, I considered myself a very healthy person. After all, I exercise regularly, am an outdoor person who eats clean, and takes health seriously. But I still got breast cancer. Ironically, breast cancer has always been circling in the backdrop, throughout my life.

I learned mammography and breast biopsy while finishing X-ray school internships, in 1990 at a local hospital. This led to a series of coincidences, that I look back at, and know this has been my niche' all along. I landed job after job that had breast cancer care involvement. It started with mammography and biopsy, then diagnostic CT and PET CT, and radiation therapy simulation, all part of my skill set. But little did I know that my radiologists' lunch seminars (in 1992) of biopsy cases matched with images, would eventually provide foundational knowledge that would be so advantageous, not only in my current career path but, later, in my personal diagnosis.

One day, not long after I entered the imaging field, my mother came in for a routine mammogram. Clearly, she had spiculation and microcalcifications present in a 1.5 cm mass. (Commonly seen as mammographic findings for malignancy). She had a stereotactic biopsy that led to a surgical biopsy finding invasive intraductal carcinoma. She chose lumpectomy and radiation at age 52. Her cancer was considered in remission, but her life was under constant enormous stress.

Fast forward to 2011. My stepbrother (ruptured aorta) and mom both passed, rather abruptly and shockingly at young ages. My stepfather was chronically ill with an organ transplant. My mom cared for him and was the primary breadwinner. So, this came as a big shock to everyone, as both their lives were cut short, passing just 3 months apart. And my mother was the matriarch of our family, an active gardener, cook, financial advisor, and always a solid foundation for advice and work ethic. I took on her role and had to establish new legal trusts for the family estate, hold estate sales, manage their medical affairs, manage their financials, move my stepdad into an assisted living community, and plan funerals. I was also in a new relationship yet had no other choice but to make family a priority. In the end, I came to learn this man was stealing from me and my family the entire time. The grief, betrayal, and loss I experienced were unfathomable. Yet, I knew I was stronger than anyone knew. I share this pivotal time, not for a pity party; but because I think the exorbitant stress and grief caused my cancer to get triggered. Yes, I had many risk factors, including genetics and never having children. But I do believe stress, to be the catalyst.

I began being super focused on my fitness and health. I started competing in spartan races and excelling at inspiring and motivating others and branding my social media presence. I was helping train people in their fitness goals. It became my drug and what fuels my fire, to this day. My first breast biopsy came after a mammogram in 2012. I was in the best shape of my life. My clean eating habits and daily sweat fest were well known. Yet here I was facing breast cancer. This biopsy revealed pre-cancer (lobular hyperplasia) so I was advised every 6 months, I should either have a mammogram or a breast MRI. And every 6 months, it was recommended I have a biopsy. This went on from 2012 to 2017. The diagnosis of lobular hyperplasia came each time. I had zero palpable masses, just "slight changes" in my imaging exams. At one point, I had 5 clips in my RT breast from each biopsy. I made a joke I would heat up on my next MRI.

In the end, I had every biopsy imaginable: MRI Guided, U/S guided, stereotactic needle biopsy, wire localization, and three surgical biopsies. On the 7th biopsy recommendation, I chose to have nipple sparring preventative mastectomies with reconstruction. That was when my MRI was abnormal once again and lit up next to the clip of a prior biopsy. Upon excision, I had lobular in situ, lobular invasive (two tumors), and one lymph node + …… YES, I too now had breast cancer!

Luckily, we have genetic testing on the tumor itself. Because it laid out the best plan of care. I was ER +, PR + (hormone receptive), and HER2 Neg. Stage 1B. Which meant I didn't need chemotherapy, or radiation but just bilateral mastectomies and hormone suppression. My preventative mastectomies became my cancer treatment plan. I had a double nipple-sparing mastectomy in August 2017, with drains in for 20 days. They expanded me for 8 weeks and

replaced my expanders with Allergen Textured Implants in Dec 2017. I had two doctors who suggested possible radiation as part of the treatment plan, stating I was in a grey area for the treatment adding much benefit. I opted not to do the radiation, as it would additionally cause a delay in my returning to work for 10 months and cause unwanted scarring.

I went back to my job of 13 years. During this time, I began noting blurred vision, rash, fatigue, memory changes, headaches, and my fingers going numb and turning white. I had some nodules on my thyroid suddenly appear. I dismissed it as aging and being perimenopausal. I also began noting my position at work was feeling "replaced". I was being almost forced out, due to strong opinions about my length of time away to tend to my health needs.

So, in Oct 2018, I resigned from my job, to preserve my good health and happiness.

Then In Feb. 2019, I had a small revision repair on the right breast for the implant dropping. I had the same plastic surgeon who did my original surgery. He made no mention of any pending recall of the implants.

In April 2019, I landed a great new job in a cancer center. I was excelling, learning radiation simulation and performing diagnostic CT. My patients loved me because of my experience, but also my gift of starting difficult IVs. My radiation therapists and radiation oncologists also connected well professionally. I was back! My big break came. I felt on top of the world to be working in my new role. Then, in July 2019, I received a letter stating my Allergen Textured Implants were recalled and could cause a rare lymphoma cancer. I was devastated to face more surgery.

I chose to wait until after I was at my job a full year to have stability, medical benefits, and disability pay. It was mentally tough, knowing I now had another type of cancer risk in my body, called BIA-ALCL. But my plastic surgeon assured me I had no physical indication of the rare lymphoma (BIA-ALCL.) So, in May 2020, I replaced my implants with silicone smooth implants. I had much debate inside my mind because I knew implants could be harmful to the body. I didn't want anything unnatural in my body. But I was single and wanted to maintain my physical body image. So, I moved forward with the implant replacement. By summer's end, I was healed on my chest but my wounds from the liposuction in my abdomen seemed to weep. The doctor's office assured me they were ok. I went kayaking and woke the next day, with a massive staph infection. This led to painfully lancing it open in the office, and 5 months of self-packing two deep wounds. They finally resolved. But I was "off" much of 2020-21. My "strange" symptoms were increasing, and I began thinking I was crazy. I felt so bad I could barely do normal life. It turns out, I was having a bad reaction (the entire time) to the foreign objects in my chest.

Yes, my implants were causing Breast Implant Illness. I found a surgeon in Michigan who specialized in such cases, and who performed an EN bloc capsulectomy explant, and full flat closure on Nov 3, 2021. Luckily, I did not have BIA-ALCL. But the implants caused an inflammatory response. (Pathology report showed chronic giant cell inflammation). To date, all my autoimmune type symptoms are gone or improving.

So, I know that having chosen keeping my overall good health, over maintaining a certain physical appearance was the greatest gift I could give myself.

Looking back, I am truly grateful for all who have influenced me; helped me physically, supported me mentally, and educated me. For without ALL this happening, I would not be here, to help other honorable women get properly diagnosed as well (and yes, a couple of brave men). I have shared this walk with my mother and wonderful friends who stood by one another, in support. Best of all, I am cancer-free, implant free, and feeling extremely healthy. I truly feel I got a second chance at life! So, at a glance, I might be flat and scarred. But my scars tell a story. They remind me of a time when life tried to break me down but failed.

Lisa is an inspiring fitness motivator, nutrition fanatic, and breast cancer survivor. On a professional level, she is a Radiological Technologist in medical imaging, specializing in Mammography, Biopsy, and CT, with a vast knowledge of breast pathology and metastatic disease. She is compassionate and kind. Helping others comes naturally and taking care of people is one of her many gifts. As a breast cancer survivor, she knows how deeply impactful breast cancer is. Her mission throughout her career has been to help women and men survive, by receiving exams for early detection, proper staging workups, and education, so they could receive the proper care to save lives.

She is so intensely passionate about helping others and living life fully. In her spare time loves skiing the mountain, spending time with animals, and boating the river.

Her take away from this walk, life is about connection and truly embracing experiences surrounding us. What once threatened our life, now brings us gifted friendships with other beautiful souls. It gives us our breath back into our lives for renewed hope and brings new positive perspectives on what is possible.

Connect with Lisa:
Facebook: www.facebook.com/lisawarzyn
email: encourage2bfit@yahoo.com

WAVE AFTER WAVE OF PINK

Positivity Heals

Tyreeanna Hoxer

When it comes to making a living, being an independent breadwinner is not easy. Art has always been a big part of my life. I love to learn new things, if I'm not learning, I lose interest and get bored. Because of this, I have developed a variety of skill sets, such as sewing and jewelry design, painting, Native American art, and some upholstery and drapery work.

Since recovering from breast cancer in 2018, I find that I enjoy being my own boss. Chemotherapy affects your body for the rest of your life, thought processing and memory never are what they once were, immunity and body pains occur all the time and you never know how you're going to feel when you wake up each day. P.T.S.D. is a given with a healthy dose of anxiety and panic attacks to endure for who knows how long if not forever. Art is my way of healing and releasing everything so I can remember to be here now and in the moment. It helps me to remember who I am and brings me back to peace. I think I get my independent spirit and thirst for knowledge from my dad. But it definitely comes with its challenges.

In 1992, my family's lives changed forever which gave us a whole new outlook on life, it molded me into the person I am today and I am grateful for the hardest of situations I've been in because it led me to people and places I never would have encountered otherwise. This is my story...

My father grew up helping in his family's upholstery and awning business, he learned to sew by watching his grandfather from his vantage point on the other side of the sewing machine and he learned to upholster furniture from his father. So, naturally, I was always drawn to sewing and working with my hands.

In 1991, my dad was an independent business owner, but he also made his living as a salesman. My mother always worked alongside my dad in the office but, at $7.50 an hour she never earned enough money to cover the mounting childcare costs for four kids. So, Mom came home full time to be with me and my three siblings. From then on, our sole income earner was Dad. He was a successful sales agent, but it was tough going in commission sales. Too often when it came to making that paycheck, it was feast or famine. They just couldn't get up on top of that steady income wave so, over time, the stress caused my parents to drink more which resulted in poor business decisions and they slowly spiraled down that economic toilet. By the Summer of 1992, they were in debt to the tune of $18,000 and were totally out of options. With no savings and no credit, they were forced to move out of our third rental home.

I was six, my brother four, and my sisters eight and thirteen. My parents didn't want us kids to be frightened or feel too much stress when we lost everything we owned and were living in our van, so they tried to turn our situation into an adventure of sorts. Our family was going to go camping! So off we all went into a completely different life and a brand-new beginning.

It was a hard time for my family, people that my parents thought were their friends shunned and turned their backs on us. There was literally only one person who was willing to help. He worked at a bagel shop and at the end of the day instead of throwing the bagels out, he gave them to us. For weeks we literally lived off of one bagel a day, half in the morning and the other half at night. my mother wrote in a journal during those times, being a mother, I couldn't imagine how hard it would have been.

We found a campground where we met other people who, like us, were just scratching to get by. People who have seen the hardest of times were the most genuine, giving people we had ever met. We were welcomed with compassion and understanding rather than ridicule and judgment. A lady welcomed us with a basket of fruit and cake from her son's birthday, and in the next few days, she taught my mom about pantries and places to go to receive help. In my mom's journal, she mentioned how grateful she was to find a woman's shelter where we all got to eat a hot meal and bathe for the first time in over a week.

From there, we became accustomed to living an off-grid nomadic lifestyle. Starting as a young child I traveled with my family. We had a Nomad trailer and later were gifted an old 1950 Chevy International school bus. This bus, however, wasn't just your average school bus, it was a chow wagon for the Grateful Dead. Full of history and named after the song Terrapin Station, it rode alongside the Further bus and was known as Terrapin Bound. It still has the original license plate that reads "Terrapin Bound, some climb, some crawl." It had taken a nosedive in the Pacific Ocean after running over a highway patrolman's car. The front end was completely rusted out, so my dad and community friends helped to fix it up and turn the bus into a rolling home. We got a 1951 Chevy front end, split the center of it, and added metal in the center to customize it to the front of the bus. From there, we stripped everything out of our nomad trailer and built it into the bus. Nobody could ever take the roof over our head again, no matter what was to come next. We had our fully functional rolling home.

I grew up in the high mountains of Ojai California, my family was adopted into Northern Cheyenne and Cherokee circles and this is a huge part of who I am and why I do the art that I do. I learned most of my skills from either my father or my adopted uncle, David Singing Bear.

Now that I have covered some of my history on how I came to be here, I will go on to the story of my breast cancer and what followed next.

In the cold winter months of November 2017, I was 31 years old and a mother of three beautiful children. I had been doing one of my passions, working as a preschool teacher for about a year and had been engaged with my youngest son's dad for seven. Life was beautiful; however, the world could never prepare me for what was to come next.

One night after a long day's work, I was relaxing when I noticed my cat Jedi was following me around everywhere and would climb onto my chest as if it were his new favorite spot and would purr constantly. I thought it was odd at first but then came to the conclusion that he was just being super sweet and snuggly during the cold change in the weather. After a few days of my cat continuing to behave this way, laying on my chest every chance he could, I remembered watching a documentary on how animals can sense things such as the supernatural and sickness in people. That's when I decided to do a breast exam. While in the shower I noticed a lump in my left breast, I was not sure if it was something that was already there so I did not think too much of it. After a few days, it was starting to weigh heavier on my mind so I brought it up to my co-worker and she insisted that I don't delay and to get in and have it looked at.

Because there had been no history of cancer in my family and due to my age, the doctors thought it was a cyst. It took almost two months to get me in for a mammogram. During those two months, I felt as if I was in a constant state of anxiety while living in the unknown. I decided to do what I do best, I buried my fears and stress, continuing to focus on my daily life.

I loved my job as a preschool teacher, it has always been one of my passions. To work with children and teach them about the world was everything to me. Spending time with babies was one of my favorite rooms to work in because I always got my snuggle fix!

Once I was able to get in for my mammogram, the doctors discovered that this was in fact not a cyst at all. They also found another lump in my other breast in the same spot and about the same size! Doctors were shocked! Those who had been working in this field their entire life had never seen anything like it. After going in for my biopsy and having blood tests drawn, it was determined that I had HER2 Positive Invasive Carcinoma in both breasts and that I also carry the BRACA2 genetic mutation.

This means that not only was cancer 100% estrogen fed, but it was also 100% manifesting on its own at a rapid rate. I was told by doctors that if I was diagnosed with this only ten years prior, it would have been a death sentence but because of new research, they discovered immunotherapy to help with the battle. I had two chemotherapies and two immunotherapies every Friday. I had a hysterectomy, a double mastectomy, and am on hormone blockers to this day.

First of all, I just want to say that I thought my tits and I were close!! Oh, how I was mistaken. Rather than be a part of me, they decided to turn against me. A dear friend/family member gave me a shirt that says "Fondle with care" and it is by far one of my favorite shirts to this day!! Every time I went in to have chemotherapy, I would wear something funny such as that.

It is so important to live life lightly and enjoy all of the little things. We are all here for a short period of time, so live it fully. I am so grateful for all of my friends and family who have rallied behind me and for everyone who supported my family and loved ones throughout those challenging times. I was so overloaded and in shock that I had a hard time absorbing information. If it was not for both of my sisters being there for me and taking notes and my mom and dad staying with me for months on end taking care of me and my children while healing from surgeries, I don't know what I would have done.

I felt numb, almost as though I had no emotion at times, I couldn't remember conversations I had or would be in the middle of talking and suddenly my brain would fart and that was that... After attending counseling, I learned that this was a normal response for people going through such trauma, it is a survival mode.

Unfortunately, I still struggle with chemo brain to this day, it never goes away. It's frustrating to others when I ask a question that they already gave me the answer to, or how I would repeat a story that they have already heard. What's even worse, it hurts my feelings because some would get mad at me and have no idea how hard it is having to be the person with the chemo brain. I'm the one who struggles with it and if it's hard on them, can you imagine what I deal with on a daily basis when it comes to simple tasks? Unfortunately, I still felt so alone even though I had so many people here for me. My relationship of seven years was over, the one person who I truly wanted to be there for me couldn't handle the stress of it all and instead drank more than ever before. I found myself in a very sad place, surrounded by overwhelming darkness that I had never known before. I stayed focused on the little light of my life that I am not yet finished living, continuing to push through that dark tunnel surrounding me of helplessness, anger, guilt, and anxiety that could so easily take control.

On March 15th after discovering cancer, I had to start my first chemotherapy session. Normally the surgeon would place a port in the chest but I got it in my arm. The port placement is done underneath the skin so that when you go in for labs and infusions, the doctor won't be required to put an IV in every time that I had to go for treatments. The needle used; I can only best describe as a very large thumbtack-like needle that plugs into the port. The nurses gave me lidocaine to numb my arm before I would come in, but I would always forget to put it on and had to just suck it up. Therefore, the ladies who worked in labs gave me the nickname "Tough Bitch."

I had my surgery for my port placement the day before my first chemotherapy. I was so sore, confused, scared and I had no idea what was going to happen. This whole world of mine turned upside down overnight and was completely out of my control. All I could think about was that I was not done with my life, I needed to raise my children and I was willing to do literally anything to make it happen. I made a choice and there was no doubt in my mind that I would beat this.

As a woman, losing my hair was one of the hardest things to go through. It is one of the ways we identify as women. I cried many times, releasing that energy of fear, pain, and sorrow that was constantly building up, then I would put one pant leg on at a time and keep moving forward. I decided that if my hair was to fall out, I was going to have it go out with a bang! So, a dear friend of the family who is an amazing barber gave me a pamper and colored my hair like a rainbow. Being a preschool teacher, the kids were thrilled when I popped into each classroom while bouncing my hair about and shouting "Look, I'm a pretty pony!"

Once my hair was starting to fall out, my sisters again, planned a day with our amazing family/barber friend Summer for a day of head shaving. That same day my pre-teen decided to get lippy with me, so I looked straight into those baby blue eyes and said "You make me want to pull my hair out!" as I grabbed a handful of the hair on my head and pulled out a huge clump. That look of utter shock was priceless and is forever seeded in both of our brains no doubt!!

While my head was being shaved, my sisters surprised me with the most beautiful and emotional moment that words cannot express. My sister Jeannie shaved her entire head and my other sister Celeste shaved the back of her head and had a pink ribbon design done on it. Family and friends created a huge event for me called "Rock for the Cause." They had live bands, raffles, and prizes to help raise money for my children and me. This was done at our favorite watering hole known as Shanahan's. That feeling of love and support I received is beyond words. I am so grateful to my family and all my friends who rallied behind me during those challenging times.

Thank you to my two sisters Celeste and Jeannie for everything you sacrificed in your lives to help me.

And, I want to mention my "adopted" big brother Turtle who I cannot thank enough for his generous gift at Christmas time 2018. What an angel this longtime friend was. Thanks to him, I was freed of my monetary stress that winter.

And thank you to both my parents John and Mary, my brother Johnny and his wife Morgan, who together held fundraiser yard sales on my behalf from their home in Arizona. My folks kept me afloat by paying my rent many times during my illness and recovery process. Thank you for camping in my driveway for nearly three months to help me on the home front before and after my first surgery. This is the kind of family that I grew up in. A family that rallies around one another not only in the good times but during the really hard times. All these people have in their own way, taught me so much. All for one and one for all. They have my undying love and appreciation. I know it was hard for them as well as me.

I had changed so much during that time and found myself looking at the world and others around me differently. I would go into the grocery store and look at people and wonder what their story was. Anyone could take one look at me and instantly make assumptions about who I am. Yet in reality, they would have never guessed that I was in pain and fighting for my life, wearing fake eyelashes, makeup to cover the redness and sores on my face, and a wig to hide from the world. I had mouth sores, bone pain, and even my fingernails were falling off due to the chemotherapy and yet somehow, I was able to find humor in almost everything. I've heard that what doesn't kill you only makes you stronger, honestly, I think it makes you funnier to boot! I was told many times that someone needs to hand me a microphone!

I grew up creating art my whole life which was how my family made a living while on the road, everything we made we would take to events such as swap meets, Saturday Market, and Farmer's Markets. My dad always said I had an eye and talent since I was quite young. I would design clothing and jewelry starting at age seven. I enjoy interacting with people and sharing what I love with the world and continue to expand my passion to this day. Before I got sick, I met a dear friend of mine named Dawn. She was running a farmer's market in 2012 when we built a friendship and she has always been so supportive of my work throughout these years while I continued to grow and expand my art. I taught myself how to paint while going through surgeries, it was and still is the best therapy I have ever known. I will provide therapy through painting and other forms of art one day. I want to utilize what I have been through to help other people to heal. I truly believe that inspiration and how we choose to think, really do impact people when it comes to the body and healing. It's been scientifically proven that stress kills. Maybe positivity heals... I sure believe it to be true.

After being in remission for about a year, my dear friend Dawn introduced me to a beautiful, strong soul. This lady has a strength that inspires many and she brings women together who live with the effects of cancer every day. There is a bond that grows between everyone and suddenly we don't feel alone and everybody starts sharing their stories. It is beautiful to be surrounded by others who truly understand what I have gone through because they too have experienced it. Her name is Deb and she runs Pink Sistas nonprofit retreat for breast cancer survivors. She taught me how to paddleboard for the very first time along with learning to kayak! It was great fun and filled with many laughs and wonderful memories!!

Life is like a spiderweb and throughout all the good and bad times in life, it leads us to people, places, and opportunities that would never have transpired otherwise. Such as myself, I would not be here writing today had I not met these beautiful people on my journey called life. I am so grateful to be here today and to have this opportunity to share my story with you. Thank you for reading and I hope this will give some inspiration and light your way.

Tyreeanna Hoxer was born in Milwaukie, Oregon and she and her family reside in Vancouver, Washington.

She loves the outdoors and is training to forage. She is learning how to identify edible, toxic, and medicinal herbs. She designs and creates jewelry, and taught herself to paint while fighting breast cancer. She plans to help others heal through art.

Tyreeanna continues to share her incredible story and plans to write a book in the near future.

Connect with Tyreeanna:
Email: Tyhoxerl986@gmail.com
Facebook: Art for the Cure: Ty's Healing Creations

WAVE AFTER WAVE OF PINK

Cancer in the Pandemic

Penda Sidibeh

On March 30th, 2020, during the lockdown, I went to the emergency department alone due to visitor restrictions; thanks to COVID19. I visited the ER Because I was beginning to have pain in my abdomen and right shoulder, especially when I breathe. I can't remember which was stronger; whether it was during inhalation or exhalation, but it was intense. With all these I didn't tell my family, my mum occasionally asked me if I was okay. My response has always been "I am fine" but I could sense that she knew what was going on in a way. Mothers' instincts, I believe.

I was scared that I had COVID. At that time everyone was scared, there were a lot of uncertainties, but I knew I needed to seek help in the hospital because the chest pain was getting stronger by the day.

Due to my chest pain, the first test they performed at the ER is EKG. The results came back as normal sinus rhythm and normal ECG. They did lab draws such as cell count, electrolytes, albumin and LDH, glucose, and blood and fluid cultures, as well as complete blood count with automated differentials. My value and the standard range were pretty normal. Troponin I was also performed and wasn't high compared to the standard value.

Now, the comprehensive metabolic panel which consists of about 17 components, revealed that some of the components were higher than normal.

The doctor did the physical examination with a chaperone present, there and then he palpated my sternum and said it could be osteochondritis. But when he palpated my left breast, he felt a large mass compare to the left one. A targeted ultrasound was performed of the right breast in the area of clinical concern at 6 o'clock and inferior to the nipple. Color Doppler was employed as appropriate.

The findings were; a poorly marginated heterogeneous solid abnormality of roughly 2.9 x 1.8 x 2.2 cm with echogenic foci, possibly calcifications, and internal vascularity, near the skin surface corresponding to the palpable abnormality.

The doctor's impression was "concern for soft tissue mass" and that the limited breast ultrasound was tailored to address the acute clinical issue, so he recommended diagnostic follow-up at a breast imaging facility for a more detailed and complete evaluation. No medication was given, however, he advised I take ibuprofen for pain management and get to a breast specialist as soon as possible.

The Mammogram and ultrasound were performed on April 14, 2020. The following day I received a letter that shocked me, and I received a call from my PCP and she recommended a core needle biopsy due to the findings that breast tissue is heterogeneously dense which may lower the sensitivity of mammography. In the right breast at 6:00 in the area of the palpable abnormality, there is a large spiculated mass which probably measures about 5 cm in maximum dimension. It contains a large group of pleomorphic calcifications centrally. It further states that in the upper inner quadrant of the right breast there is a lobulated mass with smooth borders which measures about 1.4 cm in maximum dimension and in the left breast at the 6:00 position there is a lobulated mass with well-defined borders which measures 1.6 cm in maximum dimension.

I went for the biopsy. The test was done in comparison with right breast ultrasound and diagnostic mammogram on 4/14/2020. It was so painful that the doctor could only take one sample, despite the anesthesia being increased, I refused due to the pain. A lady handed over a pink bag that read live, love, believe. She also handed me a paper that details the instructions for the aftercare.

I cried bitterly, my mother was so worried; every time I look at her, I feel sad, knowing that she wants me to be okay.

This procedure was performed on 4/21/2020. By 4/24/2020 my primary care doctor was trying to locate me. She called several times (for whatever reason, I didn't get a ring). She then was able to speak to my aunt who, called and said my doctor needs to speak to me as soon as possible. I checked my voicemail and heard a lot of messages saying that I should call back.

It was around midday April 24th, 2020 when I called her and said that she got the biopsy results and that she would like to go over them with me. She talked about fibroadenoma and then said "you have cancer". Time stopped immediately, upon hearing the word CANCER. She said she was sorry and asked if I was okay, I said yes, and then she went on about someone calling me to see an oncologist and lots more but at that point, I could only think of my mum.

When I hung up, mum immediately asked "what did they say?"
I said, well, I have cancer. I could see her face freeze, she placed both palms on her mouth. I said to her it's just cancer and I will be okay. Then I started to give her courage and said that I needed her to be strong. I called my aunt to let her know about the news and I think my uncle as well.

When I got the chance to be alone, I cried silently, didn't want her to see me sad because that will make things worse.

On 4/28/2020 I went with my aunt to see the oncology department. First, we went to get blood work done, complete blood count, and complete metabolic panel, saw the surgeon, and she reviewed her findings with me. We discussed in general, the team approach to breast cancer care. Surgical options for the breast would include; partial mastectomy followed by a course of radiation treatment, or mastectomy with or without immediate or delayed breast reconstruction through either a skin-sparing, nipple-sparing, or standard incision. Both procedures, as well as the risks including but not limited to infection, bleeding, cosmetic deformity of the breast, the potential need for additional surgery, and wound complications with mastectomies such as epidermolysis or full-thickness skin loss, were all discussed. She also reviewed the differences in terms of hospital stay, operative length, recovery, recurrence, and survival. She said I was likely a candidate for a right breast lumpectomy, pending MRI results. I have a very favorable breast size to tumor ratio for breast conservation surgery.

She said that given your young age of onset, I will likely need genetic testing. I have a very favorable breast size to tumor ratio and after workup with MRI, HER 2/neu status, and genetic testing is completed, she is hopeful that I will be a candidate for breast-conserving surgery. However, with all this, CT has to be done due to increased LFTs. She was very nice, gave me hope, and said she was looking at stage 2 breast cancer pending MRI results, and that I will be okay.

We went to see the oncologist on Tuesday, April 28, 2020 for an initial consultation. She addressed the of issue malignant neoplasm and that my cancer is very aggressive, it's called invasive ductal carcinoma (IDC), sometimes called infiltrating ductal carcinoma, and that it's very common. It began in the milk ducts and then spread to the surrounding breast tissues.

She further went on to say that I will have the surgery first, then chemotherapy because I am otherwise healthy and that she wouldn't want to expose me to harsh treatment. Which was not so bad news. She also said that the Cancer is estrogen-progesterone receptor-positive, which means my cancer is fueled by these hormones. Just before I left, she gave me another result that my cancer is HER2 negative which means that it does not contain high levels of protein; which is good in terms of treatment options and prognosis.

We went home, explained to my Mum what the doctor said and that it could have been worse, and now we are waiting to do the abdomen CT scan before they start the treatment. I did the CT on May 4th, 2020 which was on a Monday, and the following day, that doctor called me herself. She said I need to see her as soon as possible; like right now. I went with my aunt again the following day. I could see in the doctor's eyes that something terrible was wrong with my CT results. She said the surgeon called her in the evening, which she doesn't normally do, and that she had very bad news, "Do you remember the sweet girl, Penda?" she almost forgot about me, and she continued to say. "I have very bad news for you" she has liver metastasis." She said that was a shock because I look very healthy, beautiful, and fun with the little time they spent me with and that she feels so bad for me.

At that point, I wouldn't hear anything else other than "the cancer is in your liver." My world stopped, and I cried bitterly, I had a flashback of my life since I was a kid. I was afraid to die. My heart was pounding, my hands sweating, and I literally couldn't breathe. The mask I had on was wet due to the tears and nose discharge. My aunt was calming me down, with the doctor in a state of "oh God, this is hard"

The only thing I said to the doctor after she had revealed that I had metastasis breast cancer was "I don't want to die here. Please tell me how much time I have left, so that I can get on a plane and go home. I don't want my family to suffer the stress of taking a dead body back home. Please tell me."

The doctor replied "I will honor your wish Penda", and my aunt was like, "No you are not going to die now Penda", she was consoling me, but at the same time I can see that she was afraid. She asked all the necessary questions, about the chemotherapy, and the side effects, and she even asked how much time someone with this type of cancer may have. The doctor replied, "without treatment about 6 to 12months, but with treatment ... we will have to monitor and see how she responds".

Before we saw the doctor, my blood work was already taken. She sent a stat request for an echocardiogram before we start that chemotherapy to know my current cardiac status. I got a call the same day for the procedure the next day I went for the EKG.

I went to see the doctor about the results. She looked at me and asked "is there anyone with heart disease in your family?" I said my father died of a cardiovascular condition. Then she said these results show that you might not be a candidate for chemo. My aunt looked at me with her eyes wide open. I can still envision the way she looked at me, those eyes said it all. Scared, she hoped for the best but prepared for the worst. At that point, she took over the conversation with the doctor and asked the relevant questions to get as much information as she could regarding the diagnosis and treatment. All I could hear was that we will start the chemo and do an echocardiogram every 3 months. At that point, I was kind of relieved that we would at least start chemo and see the progression.

On May 8th, 2020, I went with my auntie to the doctor. She said today is the day. And since it was going to take long, my aunt went back to work and left me there. I cried when she said you are going to be okay; call me when you are ready or if you need anything or someone to talk to. I couldn't look at her, my eyes were blurry with tears. Everyone felt sorry for me; the nurses, the receptionists even some patients. At that point, the reality that I have cancer and am going to be on chemo hit me. A tall, red-haired nurse, took me to a room and said, "It's your first day, and we don't know how you will react to the treatment. If everything goes well, you will be out there", she pointed to the other side for treatment.

The pharmacist came to explain the medications and their side effects. There are side effects that most people do not experience all of. However, they are reversible and will go away after the treatment is complete. The side effects are nausea and vomiting (usually mild) diarrhea, mouth sores, arthralgia and myalgia (muscle/joint pain), peripheral neuropathy (numbness and tingling of the hands and feet), darkening of the skin, low blood pressure (occurring during the first 3 hours of infusion), and an increase in blood test measuring liver function. These return to normal once treatment is discontinued. If any of these effects persist or worsen, tell your doctor promptly. Temporary hair loss may occur. Normal hair growth should return after treatment has ended.

The nurse brought me soup noodle chicken, and some crackers, (they had stopped serving food due to the Covid 19, but she still brought the food to me, for me to feel better and have something in my system).

Throughout the IV treatment, I cried bitterly; not believing that chemo is being put inside my body to save me from premature death. At some point, I fell asleep, possibly due to the Benadryl or all of my crying. Before she put in the Taxol, she warned me that she will have to wear a gown due to its toxicity when placing it for me. I thought, "ooh, it's so toxic that she will have to wear protective gear, meanwhile it goes straight to my system". That made me cry and feel so sorry for myself.

This is the beginning of 8 months of chemotherapy, 13 months of oral chemotherapy, and radiation treatment and unfortunately, I am going back to chemotherapy treatment due to the persistence of metastasis disease. Friday 1/14/22 will be another chemotherapy journey.

Pink Sistas have availed us a platform where we can meet, eat, tell our stories, enjoy the sunshine and water, laugh, cry, and connect for a lifetime. These retreats have helped me a lot on my cancer journey.

Penda Sidibeh

Penda Sidibeh grew up in The Gambia, Africa, where she is a Physical Therapist with a Master's degree in Health Education and a Diploma in Gender and Development.

She obtained her Bachelor of Science degree from the University of Medical Sciences (Filial) in Cienfuegos, Cuba, and her Master's degree from the University of Lleida, Spain.

She has more than a decade of work experience in Pediatric, Musculoskeletal and Neurological disorders. Penda's great passion is bringing healing to her clients, sharing her knowledge to expand the field of Physical Therapy, and as well as provide community Education on Health matters.

Before traveling to Cuba to pursue a BSc degree in Physical therapy, Penda worked at the Child Protection Alliance in the Gambia as a Youth Coordinator of the Voice of the Young. She traveled through the length and breadth of the country with children to advocate for the rights and welfare of the child. This included workshops where children were invited and given a voice to speak up and speak out about matters affecting them. Her wealth of knowledge and experience is quite overwhelming, as she traversed the globe and interacted with different experts on Physical Therapy and Health Education matters. She traveled to Spain and lectured to undergraduate and Master's Students at the University of Lleida in December 2019 through the Erasmus project.

She participated in the assembly of heads of states and governments of the Organization of Africa Unity (OAU) Now Africa Unity (AU) in 2002, in Durban, South Africa.

She Co-Founded Penmar Physiotherapy and Rehabilitation clinic, in The Gambia.

In July 2020, she made a publication in the European Journal of Physiotherapy "Pain and functional limitation among rural female Gambian head-load carriers a cross-sectional study"

DOI: 10.1080/21679169.2020.1788637

She currently lives in the USA and is battling metastatic breast cancer, but this did not stop Penda from continuing to achieve her dreams. She is pursuing a distance learning Ph.D. program in the University of Lleida, Spain.

Connect with Penda
pendasidibeh6@gmail.com

WAVE AFTER WAVE OF PINK

I Thought I Was Prepared...

Erin Challenger

It was never a dull moment around my house. I was a single mom of three still at home and always on the go until I wasn't. I had started to feel like something was off with my body, but every trip to the doctor got the same results. Your bloodwork is normal; you need to lose weight and that will help the depression. Then you'll feel better. Then one day I was getting dressed and wrestling my way into my sports bra, - if you know, you know! My hand rubbed against the side of my breast, and I felt a lump. I didn't give it much thought, as I have a medical condition that causes cysts. I decided to keep an eye on it, fully expecting it to resolve on its own. But deep down I knew this wasn't going away, I knew I finally had an answer to why I just didn't feel good. I had cancer. I kept this to myself waiting to see if my intuition was right. Over the coming weeks, the lump changed, and that confirmed it wasn't a cyst. I had an appointment scheduled with my dermatologist in three weeks, so I figured while I was there and already half-naked, I would ask her to check it. She did and immediately put in a referral for a mammogram and ultrasound.

It took two weeks to get in for the tests, but on January 20, 2021, my life changed. The mammogram was completed but the doctor wanted more images, not a positive sign. Then we moved to the ultrasound. I could see the screen and knew what I was seeing was bad. The technician sent the images to the radiologist, and we waited. Then they wanted more scans and we waited again. The radiologist came in to do their own scan. This was the longest 20 minutes ever! I was by myself because of COVID, and I didn't expect any results during this appointment. I was wrong. While still laying on the exam table, exposed, the radiologist told me that the images showed that I had breast cancer. I thought I was prepared, but nothing prepares you to hear those words.

Now I had to figure out how to tell my family. How was I going to tell my kids? I had no idea how to do this. I was still in shock myself. I called my sister and my parents and told them over the phone. There were tears and a lot of questions with unknown answers. Next, I sat my three kids down and told them. I tried to prepare them as best as I could with the little information I had.

It was all very overwhelming, and that's what life would be for the year: overwhelming.

After telling my family and friends, I heard a lot of, "Let me know if you need anything" or "I'm here for you". I often said thank you because at the time I didn't know what I needed. I found myself withdrawing from people and thinking I'm on my own. My life was in chaos, and it was all I could do to get through each day one at a time. I was shutting down and unable to process anything; let alone my emotions. I felt very alone even with people. No one had gone through it and no one could truly understand. They tried and were encouraging, but if I had to hear one more time how strong I was or that I just had to be positive, I was going to lose my mind! I needed someone to say it's ok to not be ok. I needed my support team to let me fall apart, to dig beyond the surface of "I'm ok". I wasn't ok. Please, if you are someone's support team, don't be afraid to let them cry, and to allow them to grieve all that they are losing. It's ok to just be there and not say anything at all.

My dear friend, Tiffany, was my lifeline during chemo. She stepped up and offered to drive me to my treatments every other week. I didn't have to worry if I didn't feel good after or was tired; I had a way home. This gave us time to just chat about anything, not just my treatment, but how things were in her life, and I needed this sense of normalcy.

This summer I was led to the organization Pink Sistas. I attended my first retreat for women who had experienced breast cancer or were going through it currently. It was overwhelming and the tears started as my foot hit the dock. I was embarrassed and it was the first time I had really cried since telling my family. Then Deb put her arm around me and said, "this is a safe place and it's ok", and it was. I was amongst women just like me and also survivors. For that afternoon I wasn't different, and I could breathe. I could ask questions no matter how stupid they sounded, and I could tell my story and I didn't get pity but understanding. This is what I had been needing and didn't even know it.

It's almost Christmas now and I'm almost done with my radiation treatment. This is the end of so much, but I still feel so lost and unsure of everything. It's scary. I haven't heard the doctor say "you are cancer free" yet, but I'm hopeful. I know I am still a warrior and, in the end, will be a survivor. I have learned that I can't keep just going through the motions, that life is too short, and it needs to be lived!

Erin Challenger

Erin Challenger is a mom, daughter, and sister who puts family above all else. Her children bring her the most joy and are her biggest and best accomplishment.

Erin has professionally been in office administration but recently went back to school so that she could pursue what she is passionate about; helping those in need.

Growing up in Oregon, she loves to camp and paddleboard and is looking forward to venturing out again now that treatment is completed.

Connect with Erin:
Facebook: Erin Challenger

Talk to Your Family

Annie Hunnicutt

This is a story all about how my life got flipped-turned upside down... wait, that's the opening of a song, unfortunately, it is also the beginning of my journey with breast cancer.

My name is Annie Hunnicutt and, in all seriousness, this is the story of how my life was changed forever by a few words, "Tests are back and it is breast cancer." This is a story about hope, strength, change, and the importance of talking to your family and knowing your family's medical history.

About a week after my 32nd birthday, my husband felt a lump in my left breast. I was seen by my doctor a mere two days later. Due to my age, when the tumor showed up in my menstrual cycle, and a lack of family history of any breast cancer, I was told to wait 4 to 6 weeks and see if it dissipated, as it was most likely a cyst. As someone who had some years earlier had cysts on my ovaries, this sounded like the most logical thing.

In the 5 weeks that passed, the tumor grew and continued to become increasingly more painful. My doctor referred me for imaging. An ultrasound appointment was scheduled for August 15, 2017, my 8th wedding anniversary, and the last one I would celebrate. The radiologist read my ultrasound before I was allowed to leave. Pulling me into a patient conference room he said the word I had been dreading, tumor. He sent me for an immediate mammogram and told me I would need to come back in three days for a biopsy. Three days after the biopsy, I got the call. On the morning of the big eclipse, August 21st, 2017 my breast nurse navigator called with the news that I had been diagnosed with invasive ductal carcinoma and it was in at least 2 lymph nodes. I will forever be thankful to my in-laws who we were visiting in town that morning; they kept my boys busy so that we could take the phone call and figure out the next steps.

On the day of my diagnosis, my husband's aunt, after hearing about it, reached out to a friend of hers. A friend that was not only a survivor herself, but that ran a nonprofit that provides retreats for current patients and survivors. Little did I know at the time, this woman, Deb Hart, would become a wonderful friend, who would connect me to many other people I would grow to call friends and some with whom I would become incredibly close. The Pink Sistas organization has become something that is very near and dear to my heart and has inspired me to not only tell my story but to stretch my comfort zone and become who I am today.

My world, which had already been falling apart, took a major blow with that phone call. I had lost my dad unexpectedly four months earlier and my marriage had been on the rocks for some time, and now I was facing a fight for my life, a fight that I knew would be long and hard. I had a choice to make, a choice that would affect not only my then-husband, Ryan, and my two boys, Timothy age 4, and Gabriel age 2, but my mom and my sister. I could choose to allow this news to destroy me and my normal upbeat and positive personality, or I could remain positive and hopeful and surround myself with people who also spoke hope and healing. I chose to remain positive and fight this beast head-on. We canceled the marriage counseling we were scheduled to start and decided that focusing on my health was going to be the best way to hit this.

The two weeks following my diagnosis were full of tests, doctor appointments, and procedures. We met my entire care team; a medical oncologist, radiation oncologist, and breast surgeon. It was determined that I was at stage 3 and we would start 8 rounds of chemo after having a port placed in my chest, followed by a bilateral mastectomy, and then radiation. We also discovered at that time that there was indeed a family history of breast cancer on my mom's side of the family. After finding that out I had a hard time processing the knowledge that had we known about the history, imaging would have been ordered clear back in June when the tumor was first discovered. I struggled with anger at the fact that it took me getting diagnosed to find out about the other people in the family who had dealt with this devastating diagnosis.

My family, friends, church family, and the community rallied around us and did a lot of the heavy lifting for us, in many different forms. They checked on all of us, helped me with the boys, made a ton of easy fix freezer meals, took me to appointments, sent me uplifting messages, raised money for us, delivered groceries and care packages regularly, took me to appointments and the ER when I needed to go in, visited me in the hospital most of the time just sitting with me while I slept, and surrounded us with unconditional love. It was devastating and hard to have to miss my own sister's wedding because I did not feel well enough to travel to Vegas for it, but they understood and even agreed I shouldn't travel and set it up to be live-streamed so I could at least watch it live from home.

The first 2 rounds of chemo went smoothly, only feeling a bit weak and sleeping a lot more, and then came the day that I lost my hair. I thought I was prepared for it, it's just hair, but I wasn't. It hit me hard, and I ended up in tears as I buzzed it all off after it started coming out in large clumps. I realized that for as long as I could remember whenever I was feeling down on myself or needed a lift to my confidence or self-esteem I relied on my long hair or looking pretty in an outfit. It dawned on me that my hair was gone and while the original plan was to have implant reconstruction, my breasts would be scarred and would never be the same again. This realization hit me hard and I struggled to keep my positive outlook.

I did 2 more rounds of chemo before the medication changed. The new medication, Taxol, was extremely rough. I suffered from severe bone pain and dehydration (despite drinking upwards of a gallon and a half of Pedialyte and water a day). The pain landed me in the ER several times when it was not able to be controlled at home with oral pain medications. I was no longer able to drive and wasn't able to be alone with my kids due to the pain and the amount of sleep I required. Thankfully friends and family were there at every turn to pick up the slack that I was no longer able to handle. Finally, after my 3rd dose we figured out my pain could be controlled with oral pain meds if I went into the nurse's treatment room every other day for a full bag of IV fluids. With that plan, we finished out my last dose on December 27th, 2017.

On January 10th, 2018, I had a second full body scan and it appeared the disease had been fully eradicated by the chemo. We moved forward with the treatment plan and on February 1st, I had a bilateral mastectomy with expanders placed. On February 6th the pathology report came in on the breast tissue and the 21 lymph nodes that were removed and the chemo had indeed eradicated all disease from my body. All seemed to be healing well until February 27th when I went to bed at 5 pm not feeling well at all. I was nauseous and my whole body hurt. I had an event I desperately wanted to be at on the morning of the 28th, so I got up and took a hot bath, thinking that would help the body aches. I couldn't get out of the tub, and my sister had to drive over and help me. She took me to the event where I opted to use a wheelchair and then immediately following the event, she took me to the ER. I had developed a massive infection around the expander on the left side, and by 6:30 pm I was in surgery to remove the left expander and I was started on major antibiotics. A mere three days later the same signs showed up on the right side and I was again taken into emergency surgery to remove the right expander. I spent 10 days total in the hospital and had to continue IV antibiotics at home for 9 days.

In April 2018 I started radiation. In the middle of my radiation, several things in my marriage came to a head and even some discoveries were made about bad decisions I had made and it was decided we would divorce. So as not to upset my treatment I didn't move out until after the end of radiation. My 30 rounds of radiation went smoothly and I consider myself extremely lucky, as I did not have any of the bad effects that I had heard so much about. After moving out, I met with my plastic surgeon and got the news that my original plan of implant reconstruction was no longer an option after my infections. She referred me to a colleague of hers, a plastic surgeon who specializes in microsurgery and specifically DIEP (Deep Inferior Epigastric Artery Perforator) Flap reconstruction. After meeting with him I knew this was not only the surgeon for me but the correct reconstruction choice for me as well.

I was quite apprehensive after hearing and seeing both bad and good testimonies of ladies who had undergone this reconstruction. I was a single mom, who was looking at the prospect of dating life again and at the present I was not just flat but concave with excess skin on my chest after the emergency removals of the expanders, facing a 12-to-18-hour surgery that would leave not only my breasts even more scarred, but also my stomach, and there was a great possibility I would lose my nipples that my previous surgeons had worked hard to preserve for me. I went through a lot of back and forth about the surgery before it was finally scheduled for December 6th, 2018. Following my separation and ultimate divorce I had some amazing people come into my life, people who helped me decide what was going to be best for me and who put me at ease about the surgery. The reconstruction went amazingly well and I simply cannot express how thankful I am for such a great surgeon. Not only did I not lose my nipples, my scars are fading better than I expected. I did develop an infection in my abdomen at 5 weeks post-op that landed me back in the hospital for 3 days, but we caught it a lot earlier than the previous time and it was cleared up easily.

Right before my reconstruction surgery, I had the privilege of being asked to join Deb on the first-ever Winter Pink Sistas retreat up on Mt. hood. It was exactly what I needed, when I needed it. The group of ladies I was with was fun, inspiring, and so nice. We all had a great time bonding over activities, meals, walks, and visiting.

I am now three years out from my reconstruction, I feel beautiful, strong, and healthy. There is always the fear of the return, but I go in for my regular checks and have decided not to live my life in fear. I have become more physically active, taking up kayaking with my boys in the summer, and various arts and crafts all year long. I try to eat healthily, but I still enjoy the things I like such as cheesecake and ice cream, just in moderation. I learned the importance of self-care, self-love, and being an advocate for yourself; whether that be with medical staff or in friendships and relationships. I have decided to live my life and enjoy it. I have learned how strong I truly am, not only physically, but mentally and emotionally as well, and I am proud of the person I have become through this trial and journey with breast cancer.

The last thing I want to touch on is something that has become my platform, so to speak. Talk to one another. Talk to your family. I encourage everyone to make sure they have a solid knowledge of their family medical history, because had I known what I know now, my disease maybe could have been caught and treated before stage 3. Because they had to remove so many lymph nodes I now fight with lymphedema and probably always will. Had the cancer been diagnosed earlier (I do not blame medical staff as it didn't make any sense at my first appointment to assume tumor or cancer), nodes wouldn't have been involved yet and this most likely wouldn't have been something I would have to deal with. So please, talk to one another, talk to your loved ones.

Annie Hunnicutt

Annie Hunnicutt is a kayaker, all-around country girl, and avid crafter. Her passion is being creative and connecting with people on a real level. Annie is a Production and Supply Shop Planner but has a unique ability to find and connect with people in the communities that she loves; the breast cancer community and the veteran community.

As a mom of two small boys, she has learned the value of deep and lasting relationships and having a solid support system. On top of being a mom and holding a full-time career, she has recently put her love of crafting and arts to work for her and has started a fiber arts store with her mom. She spends her free time with her boys and those she loves and considers family.

Connect with Annie:
Facebook: Annie Marie Hunnicutt
Facebook page: Prairie Fiber Arts.

WAVE AFTER WAVE OF PINK

I Did Not Feel Sick
Paige Hairston

I will start from the very beginning. On January 31st, 2020, I found out I had cancer in my left breast. I was in complete shock and sad because I did not feel or look sick, but there I was sick with breast cancer.

As soon as I got off the phone with the nurse navigator, I called my husband and he immediately started tearing up over the phone. That was when I started crying too. He came home and we cried and hugged and cried again then we proceeded to make the plans for my treatment. We Face-Timed all 4 of our daughters and each call broke my heart over and over again.

I had surgery on February 24th, 2020, and had the mass removed, 12 lymph nodes, and a tumor that was the size of an egg from my upper left back (that was benign). Three days later I received a call from my breast surgeon with the news that unfortunately, I had a cancerous tumor in one of my sentinel nodes. This meant that I was now a Stage 2 and would need a PET scan and chemotherapy.

The PET scan was to see if the cancer had spread to any other parts of my body. She continued to say that she was not sure how much chemotherapy I would need, but I was most definitely going to need it because of the lymph node involvement.

This was all only 3 days post-surgery and I was in shock because this was of course, unexpected and to be honest, I was just tired and sad.

About a week later after the PET scan, I got the good news that the PET scan came out clean, but my Medical Oncologist still recommended chemotherapy for 3 months, once every 3 weeks, followed by 5 to 6 weeks of radiation.

I recovered from surgery and in March of 2020 I started chemotherapy.... well, let's just say that this was just something I would love to forget and not go through again. When I started losing my hair I cried, when I completely lost it, I cried. Since there was Covid and no one else could go anywhere and have fun, I guess you could say that was a good time to go through treatment???

I don't know; all I remember is that I swore to myself that if I ever felt better, which I knew would happen, I would have as much fun as I possibly could within reason and affordability. I promised myself that I would travel more and take better care of my body and do the things I really loved and tell people my true feelings …honestly. I promised myself all these things while looking out the window at my neighbors and the trees and people walking by. I promised myself even more as I endured each round of chemotherapy with a smile. I also promised myself to not be afraid of letting go of people that didn't deserve to be in my presence, and hold myself to higher standards, do what I want to do, and not hold grudges.

Fast forward to tonight at 8:51 pm December 31st, 2022. We are a few hours away from the new year. As I write this and look back on all the photos of myself and all that I have done since my January 2020 diagnosis, I can't help but be grateful – thankful - that I am still here. I am doing the things that I love and trying my best to honor the promises I made to myself.

It will be exactly two years in January 2022 that I will be in remission from breast cancer. Are there some setbacks? Of course, there are, but because of this journey, I am stronger, wiser, and know what I want and what I don't want more than ever.

I am continually evolving because of the journey I am on and that is ok. Honestly, I am just happy I have a full head of hair on my head and am healthy and doing things that I love. I feel like I am braver than I was before and way more forgiving, upfront and transparent.

Because of this journey, I am more selfish with what I want, my time, and my life. I love the fact that I am truly evolving and am staying true to the things I want. Thank you for reading this and I do hope my story inspires you and brings you joy. :)

Paige Hairston

Paige is a married mom of 4 daughters living in Portland, OR. She and her husband have been married for 29 years and their daughters are ages 28, 26, 24, and 21. Paige attended Portland State University for her undergraduate and Master's Degree and teaches college classes at Mt. Hood Community College and Warner Pacific University.

Her hobbies involve running outside, attending Bodycombat and Zumba classes, reading, shopping, Karaoke, and cooking. She also loves bike riding around her neighborhood and attending brunch with friends.

Paige was born and raised in Los Angeles, California, and moved to Portland to attend college and graduate school.

Paige is a very social person and loves making new friends and going for long walks while catching up with family and friends. She also likes to play golf with her husband and other fun ladies who like to golf. She is a lover of life and seeks to continue to grow both mentally and emotionally.

Connect with Paige:
paigewhairston@gmail.com

Is This What I Think It Is?

Becci Owens

It was Rose City Comic Con Weekend in Portland, a big deal in my house. My husband and son are both comic book geeks. We all went down to the Convention Center for the Con that Sunday, January 25, 2015. I was feeling kind of off all day. You know the feeling like you might be coming down with a small virus or something. I brushed it off as nothing and tried to enjoy the day with my family.

The next morning though, as I was getting ready for work, I put my bra on and stuck my hand down the side of my right boob to adjust it in the bra (as I'm sure we've all done a time or two). I will never forget it. I felt a lump. Not just a tiny little pea-sized lump. This lump was about the size of a nickel and quite noticeable to the touch. When did this show up? Why had I not felt this before? Is this really what I think it is?

I decided to just go on with my day and try not to think too much about it until I got home from work. That's when I had my husband come up to our room and feel it. I first had him feel the left breast, then the right. He looked at me and said, "Oh, that's not right. You need to call the doctor tomorrow and have that checked." That's when the fear really started to kick in. My stomach was turning, I didn't sleep all night, I just couldn't get my brain to stop going to the worst outcome.

Tuesday morning, January 27, 2015. I went to work, never told a single soul what I had found, and waited for my doctor's office to open so I could call and get an appointment to be seen. I found an empty board room and closed the door. I nervously dialed and waited for the front desk to answer. When she did finally answer, I told her who I was, who my doctor was, and that I had found a lump in my right breast. She asked if I could be in the office in twenty minutes.

"Of course!"

I told a coworker I had an emergency appointment and would be back, and out the door I went. I was trying so hard not to cry the whole drive to the doctor's office. Once there, they put me in an exam room, had me put on a gown, and then the doctor and his nurse both came in for the exam. I love my doctor ... he's amazing. He was so calm about the whole thing. He had me lay back with my arm over my head, closed his eyes, and started his exam on the left boob. He kept his eyes closed and moved over to the right boob.

As soon as his fingers came to the lump, his eyes opened. He looked at me and said, "That's it, isn't it?" I answered, "Yes." He assured me that it was probably nothing but wanted to send me in for a mammogram-it had been two years since I'd had one-to be sure. I had my mammogram two days later. They didn't like what they saw, so I was then scheduled for a biopsy.

Tuesday, February 3, 2015. Today was biopsy day. I was terrified, to say the least! My husband went with me for support, the first of many appointments he'd be attending with me. He was able to be in the room with me during the biopsy. I remember being so grateful for that. He held my hand. I cried. He gently wiped my tears. They took a biopsy of the lump on my breast, as well as an inflamed lymph node under my right armpit. They placed tiny titanium markers at the same time. They sent me home with an ice pack under my arm, advised me to take some Tylenol for the pain, and said the doctor would call with the results. Then came the waiting game. The worst game ever!!

Friday, February 6, 2015. The answer was in. I got the call from my doctor that evening. I'll never forget it. He sounded devastated. "I am so sorry to have to tell you this, but the biopsy results came back showing that you have metastatic, poorly-differentiated carcinoma. It's triple-negative breast cancer, and it's also in the lymph node that was biopsied."

I was forty-three years old. My husband and nineteen-year-old son sat on the couch in the living room watching my face while I got this news, all the while wondering what the doctor was telling me. I wrote it all down, thanked the doctor, went and sat on the couch with my husband and son, and cried, while telling them, "I have cancer." My entire world had just changed, and I had no idea how big of an impact it was going to have on my life, on our life, going forward. This was the day the whirlwind truly started.

I was blessed with a doctor who had connections to some of the most amazing and best doctors in the Portland area. The ball was rolling, and it was rolling quickly! I met with my surgical oncologist, my medical oncologist, and the genetics counselor the very next week. We decided to have a port placed so as to save my veins. My port was placed on February 18, 2015, and I started my first of eight ACT chemo infusions on February 20, 2015. Everything was happening so fast, I felt as if my head was up in the clouds and I was watching my life happen from afar.

Chemo sucked ... it truly sucked. I was sick, I lost my hair, and I had no appetite. My taste buds changed and everything tasted metallic. I had mouth sores. I had bone pain. I had the hand-foot syndrome. My eyes and nose wouldn't stop watering. My blood counts would plummet, and I ended up requiring two or three blood transfusions in addition to the chemotherapy. I was so exhausted and overwhelmed from it all. If I wasn't sleeping or puking, I was crying. I cried a lot!

I finally finished chemo (or so I thought) on May 28, 2015. One month later, on June 25, 2015, I had my bilateral mastectomy. During the surgery, they removed seventeen nodes from my right arm (five were positive for cancer) and they found two more tumors in my right breast for a total of three tumors. Tissue expanders were also placed for future reconstruction. I had to go back into surgery about a week later for a revision due to one of the incisions not wanting to heal properly and the skin was dying off. Once I had completed the painful healing from the surgery, it was back to four more rounds of chemotherapy infusions. This time it was carboplatin. My oncologist said this was to mop up anything microscopic that may have been left behind. So, four rounds, and I was done with chemo. Then on to radiation therapy.

Radiation started in November of 2015. I had twenty-six days total, including Thanksgiving Day. My last day of radiation was December 11, 2015, and I couldn't have been happier! My skin was literally burned from my chest through to my back and under my armpit. I was one giant, horribly blistered sunburn. But I was done!

On May 12, 2016, I got my reconstruction. I was so excited! Away with those horrible expanders and hello Betty and Veronica! It was a pretty easy recovery. I only took a week off of work and was back at it again. Taking it easy, of course, but happy to be able to get back to at least somewhat of a normal life. In August we welcomed our goofy dog Mod into the family. It was a good year.

2017 started out pretty great. Work was going well for both of us, our son was doing well in his job, we moved to a new house in a neighborhood we've always loved, and then I found it. Yes, again I found a lump. It was in the same place as the first lump in 2015. I was devastated. I was actually at a follow-up appointment with my reconstructive surgeon and asked about it. He wasn't sure what it was, so he sent me down to get an ultrasound-literally minutes later. I went back on my own while my husband waited in the waiting room. They started the ultrasound and told me it didn't look like scar tissue, but they weren't sure what it was.

I knew. In my gut, I knew. I asked, "You're going to have to do a biopsy, aren't you?" They told me yes, so I asked if they could bring my husband in. They asked his name and went out to get him for me. As soon as I saw him walk in, I burst into tears. My gut was right.

On June 26, 2017, just two years and one day from the date of my bilateral mastectomy, I got the biopsy results. The cancer was back. It was a local recurrence, meaning it was in the same place and hadn't spread. Thankful for that but pissed that it was back, we knew what we had to do. We'd done this before and knew what to expect.

Chemotherapy started again in July 2017. This time was a combination of capecitabine and gemcitabine. There went my hair again and here came the side effects. Nausea, achiness, and loss of appetite are all the fun things that come with it.

My tumor showed zero response to this chemotherapy thanks to the fact I also have Stage 4 kidney disease due to a strep infection when I was a teenager.

In October 2017, I went back into surgery to have the tumor removed. Unfortunately, it was discovered the tumor had attached itself to the capsule around the implant, so my surgeon wasn't able to get the entire tumor during that surgery. I had to go back a couple of weeks later and have the remainder of the tumor, the capsule, and yes, the reconstruction removed. I went ahead and had her remove both Betty and Veronica because, well, they just had to stick together. I was upset, for sure.

Not only had I lost my real boobs, but now I've lost the replacements as well. After having the drains from the surgery removed, I ended up with a pocket of fluid that kept needing to be drained. After weeks of going in twice a week to have it drained, back into surgery I went. The surgeon removed the pocket (a seroma) and stitched my skin down so that it had nowhere to come back to.

The next step was Xeloda. What a horrible drug! My hair grew back (extremely curly this time), but I think I had the worst case of hand-foot syndrome there ever was! My hands and feet were so swollen, red, itchy, and flaky. My palms and the bottoms of my feet literally looked and felt as if I had set them in the bottom of a searing hot frying pan. The burning feeling was unbearable at times. It hurt to walk. I would work at home just so I didn't have to hobble through the office at work because my feet were so tender to walk on. I was on the Xeloda until April of 2018 and celebrated after that last dose. I was so happy to be done with it!

Life was going back to normal again. In June 2018, I heard about a private gym and trainer just down the street from my house who was offering a six-week fitness challenge. I joined to try to get myself back into a healthier condition.

I started out slow, working out for thirty minutes, three days a week. After a few months, I had worked my way up to thirty minutes, five days a week. My self-esteem was booming; I was losing weight and inches and feeling fantastic. In October I had a PET scan to follow up after the Xeloda treatments. I got the call on October 18, 2018. I was N.E.D.! (No evidence of disease.) I cried with excitement. I never thought I'd hear those words. Unfortunately, they were short-lived.

In February 2019, I had another follow-up PET scan. I was expecting it to come back clear as well, but I was wrong. Very wrong. The cancer was back. It was metastatic to the left lung.

My world came crashing down. Here we go again. I'm in treatment again with no timeframe on how long it will be. My doctors have asked if I want to see a counselor or if I am a part of a support group at all. I have always avoided support groups since I have such great support from family and friends.

Pink Sistas

That is until I heard about Pink Sistas. I saw that they had an opening for their winter 2019 retreat. I contemplated whether or not I should try to go. I made the jump and called. I was in! I went to the retreat and am so happy I did!

I met so many amazing women who will forever be in my heart. I only wish that I had heard about Pink Sistas in 2015 when my first diagnosis came. They are amazing and a wonderful form of support! They will be the first bit of information I give to anyone I meet who is just being diagnosed.

I am still going to the gym three days a week, working full time, and loving life. I try to keep everything positive and ignore any negative. This disease is a true beast! I have faith though that God knows what my future is and with the help of my family, friends, and now my Pink Sistas, I can do anything I put my mind to. I love you, Pink Sistas!

The End of the Story...... By Jim Owens

Becci's cancer continued to grow and spread. When it came back for the third time, it had developed in her right lung and she started a new chemo that would cause her to lose all use of her right hand and arm. Being the fighter she was, she just marched on to the next treatment refusing to slow down or give cancer an inch.

Unfortunately, the cancer continued to grow and spread out from her lung to her liver, bones, and finally, her brain. We had no idea it had traveled so far. One night while watching football she forgot who she was, where she was, or who anyone around her was. Thinking she had had a stroke an ambulance rushed her to the hospital only to discover 42 tumors in her brain. The doctors didn't think she would survive the night but in true Becci fighting spirit, she not only made it through the night but started to remember who she, and everyone else was. She immediately had gamma knife surgery to remove 15 of the tumors and started another round of chemo followed by 12 straight days of full brain radiation.

At the end of November 2021, the doctors told Becci that there was nothing else they could do since the cancer had become too aggressive and she would be entering an in-home hospice. The staff lined up to hug her one by one, tell her how impressed they were with how hard she had fought for so long, and cry with her.

Becci spent less than two weeks on in-home hospice. Never willing to give cancer an inch of her spirit on Friday, December 3rd, 2021 Becci was talking about what our plans would be for next Christmas, are we spending it at home or going to go to her parent's house? On December 7th, 2021, just 4 days later Becci passed away at home surrounded by family and friends that loved her more than words could ever express.

Becci was my wife for 28 years, my best friend for 30 years, and the perfect mother of our son. She was an amazing human being with the biggest heart and strongest spirit I have ever encountered. My life, as well as all the people she touched throughout her life, will never be the same again.

In Memoriam...

Becci Owens

More about Deb Hart and Pink Sistas

Pink Sistas has been helping women for 10 years as a 501(c)3 non-profit corporation dedicated to raising funds for no cost retreats for women who have been diagnosed with breast cancer.

As the founder of Pink Sistas Inc., Deb Hart is an inspirational speaker, mother, mentor, friend, breast cancer survivor, and breast cancer survivor confidant.

FUN at NO cost! Pink Sistas day retreats are focused on healing and learning to have fun after a diagnosis of breast cancer.

The day retreats consist of opportunities for paddle boarding, kayaking, yoga, socializing with other cancer fighters, and going on a party barge ride in our pinked-out boat. These day retreats provide an irreplaceable safe place where women can find comfort and light, and sometimes, life-long friendships.

Leave the cancer diagnosis at home, and come to the river for some FUN on The Pink Drifta!

This great work could not be carried out
without the help of our dedicated board members:
Annie Hunnicutt
Bradley O'Neil
Tami Marie Starkey
Kristine Canham

Connect with Deb:
Email: inspirationaldebhart@msn.com
Facebook: Pink Sistas, Inc.
Website: https://pinksistas.org

It's Fine, I'm Fine, Everything is FINE!

Danielle Cooper

I can't remember the woman I was before I got breast cancer. Based on pictures and social media posts, I was a naïve, 28-year-old mom of one, wife to my high school crush, (though we didn't date until 7 years after we graduated high school) and on a career track I had worked my butt off for. I had amazing family and friends. My husband and I had dreams of having a large family. I was doing all the right things, but I was also lost, unconfident and self-deprecating. The woman I described feels like a complete stranger to me now. How does this happen? How have I changed so much in 5 years that when I look at pictures of me prior to my diagnosis I barely recognize the woman looking back at me? Let me tell you.

Cancer was the last thing on my mind when I would do self-breast exams every few months; it was just something I was taught I should do once I had boobs. But in February 2016, I actually felt something for the first time in all of those years of hap-hazardously doing these self-breast exams. The lump was the size of a dime, hard, and my stomach fell to the shower floor the minute my fingers grazed it. I felt sick but quickly told myself to get it together. None of my blood relatives had breast cancer so there was no way at 28 years old I would have breast cancer. I abruptly exited the shower, grabbed my phone, and Googled "What does breast cancer feel like". I then spent about 15 minutes, dripping wet, going from one site to another, changing up the way I asked the question on Google, before concluding, that I was in fact too young for breast cancer. I decided I needed to push that idea to the very back of my brain because it was RIDICULOUS! Nevertheless, each month I would continue to feel that lump get a little bit bigger, usually after my period, and each month with a sick feeling in my stomach, I would tell myself it was all in my head.

Flash forward about 4 months, it was Mother's Day. My husband and I had woken up and were chatting in bed when I asked him why my boobs were so lumpy. He proceeded to give me this diatribe of how muscles can sometimes feel lumpy and that I was right hand dominant, I cut him off, grabbed his hand, and informed him that my right boob is super lumpy! The words that came next caught me so off guard that I'm surprised I didn't drive to the urgent care for an exam at that moment, "Danielle, that's cancer you need to have that looked at!" The ironic thing is he was 100% joking, he had no way of knowing that it actually was cancer. I batted his hand away and told him how ridiculous that was and off we went for our Mother's Day adventure!

One of my superpowers is the ability to compartmentalize things so that they don't have the power to cripple me with anxiety so that Mother's Day wasn't cluttered by my overactive imagination coming up with all sorts of doom and gloom, I just had fun. Unfortunately, that night while sleeping my imagination worked overtime in my dreams, urging me to go see a doctor about this growing lump that I was now convinced was cancer. I ended up going to work that next day, riddled with anxiety and sleeplessness. This wasn't my normal anxiety, this was a pit in my stomach, a bad taste in my mouth, and an inability to focus type of anxiety. It ended up driving me straight to my naturopathic doctor. She was about to enter into an appointment but something in my eyes told her to see me anyways. She kindly told me she didn't think it was anything to worry about but to put us both at ease I should go have a mammogram, a referral was immediately faxed over and I called the imaging clinic to schedule my mammogram before pulling out of her parking lot.

"Hello, scheduling how can I help you?" Said the woman at the Imaging clinic.

"Hi. My doctor just sent over a referral for a mammogram and I'm hoping I can get that scheduled at your next earliest opening."
"Okay, can you give me your full name and birth date?"
"Danielle Cooper, June 29th, 1987"
Sighing the woman on the line says, "I'm sorry, why do you need to schedule a mammogram? You are too young."
Frustrated by her attitude I say, "Well, ma'am, I have a lump so my doctor wants to have it imaged."
"Well, I can't schedule you for a mammogram." She now sounds completely exasperated by my insistence to be scheduled.
"Okay..." I say with as little irritation as I can keep out of my voice, "Well if you won't schedule me for a mammogram and I have a lump and need it imaged what can you schedule me for?"
"Well, I guess I can schedule you for an ultrasound. Do you have a family history of breast cancer?"
"No, I don't have a family history, just a lump and you should definitely schedule me for that ultrasound."
"I'll have to send in a request for another referral from your doctor and if it doesn't get approved, you'll have to pay out of pocket for the ultrasound. Do you still want to schedule it?"
"Yes, your next earliest opening please."

As I hang up from the world's most frustrating call with a scheduler, all I could think was, am I crazy? I am young and all the women I've ever known who had breast cancer were over 40 and those very few instances I had heard of young women getting breast cancer were because of the BRCA gene. I drove home, working hard to convince myself that it couldn't be cancer through the use of my personal mantra, "It's fine, I'm fine, everything is FINE!".

Three days later, on May 12, 2016, everything changed.

You never expect it to be you. We watch people on TV, in movies, and in books get diagnosed with cancer and it seems like such a whirlwind. You never know until you are on the receiving end of that diagnosis how unique every situation and diagnosis is. The radiologist, who kindly told me the day of my ultrasound that she knew it was breast cancer, told me a week later, after multiple failed attempts to get an appointment that wasn't a month from the day I got my biopsy results back, that "breast cancer isn't considered an emergency" ...WHAT IN THE ACTUAL HELL! I am 28 with a one-year-old son, husband, family, career and you are telling me my cancer can wait because it's not going to kill me today! This is in fact a GOSH DAMN EMERGENCY TO ME!! Luckily, that amazing radiologist not only spoke the truth about the lack of urgency around a breast cancer diagnosis in young women but also advocated for me and got me in to see both a Surgical and Medical Oncologist at Compass 2 weeks later.

The entire experience from diagnosis until that first appointment was like a dream. My compartmentalization super-power paid off in dividends because while everyone around me was losing their mind over my diagnosis, I was just ready to get busy beating cancer's ass. Between telling close family and friends of my diagnosis, comforting people who thought it was helpful to cry or tell me stories of their "aunt" who had cancer, I shut the emotion and fear in a closet, knowing at some point I'd need to deal with it, but not being ready in that moment. I needed to be strong. I had to be strong. So, I repeated my mantra "It's fine, I'm fine, everything is FINE! Obviously, that was just a coping mechanism.

On the day of my first visit to Compass Oncology, I was so nervous that I actually spent most of the appointment trying to make jokes, giggling like I was high, and walking around with a fake ass smile. I'm sure the nurse who took my vitals had someone paged in case I lost it. I can't imagine what my husband was thinking but I'm glad he just let me act crazy. My surgical oncologist, Dr. De La Melena at Compass Oncology West, was so comforting, smiled, and answered all of my husband and my questions. She laughed at my ill-timed jokes and validated my fears. In honesty, it wasn't the appointment with her I was worried about, I already knew I wanted to get a double mastectomy. It was the medical oncologist I didn't want to see.

The amount of information and paperwork I was given that day was ridiculous. What was even more ridiculous was being told, not asked, when I needed to be at these appointments for my breast MRI, my PET scan, for my port placement surgery. I believe I said "I have a job, I don't have time for this, I have a life..." more times than my husband or care team could count that day. I was given the times for my pre-chemo lesson, it was the only time I was given options for appointments, with my medical oncologist's Physician Assistant. Then my Medical Oncologist, Dr. Jay Andersen, gave me my treatment plan...

- 8 rounds of chemo, every 2 weeks
- Chemo would be split evenly between AC (Adriamycin) and Taxol
- Monthly Zoladex shots to completely shut down my reproductive organs and officially put me in menopause
- 4 weeks after my last chemo I would have my bilateral mastectomy
- 5-10 years of hormone-blocking medication starting immediately after my mastectomy
- 6 weeks of radiation, Monday through Fridays, starting roughly 4 weeks after my mastectomy
- 6 rounds of Zometa infusions every 6 months to reduce my risk of reoccurrence in my bones

I know some cancer treatments do make people very, very, sick, I was lucky. I was so determined that cancer would not get to call the shots and run my life that I tracked every single side effect from that first treatment and reported back immediately to make sure that what could be corrected by pre or post-drugs was. I also was avid about seeing my naturopath for fluids and vitamin infusions, like the ones people in Europe get to help their bodies recover. I also saw my acupuncturist multiple times a week to combat neuropathy, bone pain, nausea, constipation, diarrhea, etc. I started losing my hair 15 days after my first treatment, 2 days later I asked my husband to buzz my hair, 3 days after I shaved my head, I turned 29 years old and I was almost completely bald, it was rough. I had been so successful in keeping the major side effects of chemo at bay, but my naturopath and acupuncturist couldn't keep me from losing my hair.

Cancer got to take some things from me, like my hair and breasts, but I refused to let cancer dictate our life, so I asked my husband to keep his normal work hours, just as long as he could be with me on treatment days and the Sunday after treatment, which were always my hardest days. I also asked him not to quit playing in his summer adult baseball league. I wanted life to be as normal as possible. I refused to stop working, and am so glad I did because working became a safe haven for me, a place I could escape my cancer. Don't get me wrong, it was hard. What made it less hard was all the support and help from family and friends. Here's a list of all the ways my tribe of family, friends, and coworkers helped us that summer:

• My two best friends and I would go to dinner at least once a week and one or both would stay to make sure I got our son to sleep before giving me a hug filled with so much strength and love that it would carry me into the next day.

• My sister-in-law would come over at the drop of a hat to help me with our son.

• My dad would take our son every Saturday to let me rest, while my husband worked or played baseball.

• My coworkers rallied around me, giving me care packages and gift cards so that my husband and I could go out.

• My mom continued to watch our son and keep him late if I needed to go to my naturopath or acupuncturist.

- My grandparents would come to take me to appointments, clean our house and take me to dinner so I could get out of the house.
- My in-laws would come over to the house after they got off work to play with our son so I could sleep and rest after a long day at work.

Even with all of that help and support, that summer was undeniably hard. One of my best friends had a miscarriage almost a month after my first chemo and we spent most of July just sitting outside watching my son play in his little kiddy pool, not talking, but just being there for the other. Sometimes she and I would reflect back on a trip we'd taken at the end of April, before all of our individual issues were even a thought in our mind, and laugh at those naïve stupid girls who were blissfully unaware of the pain they were about to walk into. I mean the other shoe drops at some point, right? It was a dark time.

In the initial parts of my diagnosis, I really didn't know anyone else with cancer. I didn't go to support groups and while I followed a few young women with breast cancer on Instagram, it took me almost 5 months to finally meet someone in my area who'd gone through treatments, who was my age. I was lucky to find her as ultimately, she was the one that invited me to a Pink Sistas retreat. It was through that retreat that I was able to really embrace the "good" things that came with my diagnosis. Community, support, love, compassion, understanding, and friendship. Those are all the things that Deb Hart, founder of Pink Sistas, brings to each of her retreats and the bonds that you forge with the women you meet through her are irreplaceable. Being able to find community during all of this was definitely something that I will be able to hold on to for the rest of my life, along with the memories I made during the Pink Sistas retreat I attended a little over a year after my diagnosis.

However, where there is good, there is also bad, or shall I say hard.

One of those hard things, that I was completely unprepared to deal with, was the impact my diagnosis had on our son. There would be evenings when he would cry for an hour after my mom dropped him off at home. For the first time, I felt like he didn't want anything to do with me. It was hard seeing the look in his eyes when I would take off my hat, headscarf, or wig. It's one thing to not recognize myself in the mirror but to know my own son doesn't recognize his mama is like a thousand knives in your heart. I was told that our son wouldn't remember anything about this time and that it wouldn't have any lasting effects on him because he was too young. I'm here to tell you that 5 years after my diagnosis our son still remembers that it made him sad and scared when I didn't have any hair and was sick. Luckily, we've mended our relationship and he no longer looks at me with fear in his eyes, but I'm sure he will carry that trauma with him for the rest of his life. I was blessed that by the time I had my DIEP Flap Reconstruction, at the end of 2017, he was old enough to comprehend that mama had ouchies on her chest and that he needed to be super careful around me. He would help me walk to the bathroom, holding my hand the short walk from my recliner to the bathroom, and wait for me to finish before walking me back to my recliner. I truly feel that his ability to help and be present during my recovery from that surgery helped him process what was happening in a much healthier way, ultimately helping us to repair the bond that was so tragically broken during the year prior.

Overall, my surgeries were varying degrees of difficult. I had my bilateral mastectomy in October 2016 and besides horrible constipation and nausea from the anesthesia, it was relatively painless. Probably because my body was so beat down and numb from chemo, but I decided that it was a win. Especially because I'm a unicorn and always have weird complications/issues, here's a shortlist of the ones that cropped up following my mastectomy:

- My right expander had a hole in it and deflated within 4 hours of it being placed, over the muscle, during my mastectomy. This required another day in the hospital and another surgery to replace it and put a new one in.
- My post-mastectomy pathology on the tumor that was still nestled in my breast tissue showed that I was in fact not just ER/PR+ but HER2+. This not being captured during my biopsy back in May was considered an anomaly. It required a complete change to my diagnosis and treatment plan and added 18 Herceptin infusions and 6 Projeta infusions over the course of the following year.
- Roughly 5 months after my mastectomy I was diagnosed with red breast syndrome. Apparently, I'm allergic to AlloDerm, the dehydrated sheet of sterile tissue that is donated from human (and sometimes animal) cadaver skin which is used to encapsulate the expanders/implants so that they don't move around in your chest. Redbreast syndrome is when the AlloDerm breaks down due to an allergy and basically turns your breast into a red-hot ball of fluid. This sealed the deal on my reconstruction options. I could either go flat or have DIEP Flap Reconstruction.
- Roughly 8 months after my DIEP Flap Reconstruction and 4 months after my fat grafting revision surgery I was diagnosed with postoperative pressure ulcers on my left breast, which, left me scarred and unable to continue having revision surgeries due to the risk of losing my left flap tissue.

DIEP Flap Reconstruction is a no-nonsense surgery. It takes between 12-and 16 hours for the surgeon to remove the tissue from your abdomen, preserving the main blood vessels that he'll use to connect it to your chest wall, and then carefully re-attach these vessels and validate that they will survive. From there it's up to 5 days in the hospital so that you can be monitored hourly for any blood flow issues to the flap. You aren't allowed to lay down for 8 weeks and it gives you a scar that runs from one hipbone to the other. I don't remember much from that surgery or the recovery over the following couple of weeks. Again, my amazing tribe of family and friends rallied around me. My grandmother spent every day with me, making me food, keeping me company while I watched endless amounts of Netflix, and allowing our son to stay home with me during my recovery. She was definitely the MVP during that time and I will never forget how much support she gave me during that time. My grandfather made countless trips up and down I-5 driving me to and from post-op and acupuncture appointments. I'm still in awe of the support my husband, our son, and I have received during these hard times, and will never stop thanking God for every person that helped us get through these ridiculously hard times.

Overall, in the last 5 years, I've evolved from a naïve, physically healthy woman who lacked confidence and routinely trashed her body, to become a sick, bald, fearful woman with triple-positive stage 2B breast cancer who mistrusted her body. Finally evolving into a healthy and happy woman who has grown exponentially and has found peace and love for the body that birthed an amazing child and beat cancer. Cancer is horrible, it truly is, but the lessons and growth I was able to take from cancer are something I cherish. My journey with breast cancer reminds me of a tree in a forest, tall with lush, green overgrowth surrounding it, seemingly full of life, perfect. Then a fire cuts through the beauty, scarring the tree and killing the overgrowth surrounding it. A man rushes in to extinguish the fire but the damage is done, the tree is badly scarred and looks like it may die. But it doesn't die, it continues to live and over time, people begin to see that the fire that they thought ruined and nearly killed the tree actually helped the tree to release seeds that are sprouting new growth, more beautiful growth, and we stop mourning the scars from the fire and instead see the blessings it brought the forest.

Danielle Cooper

Danielle Cooper is a Stage 3b Triple Positive Breast Cancer Thriver who routinely shares her journey through motherhood, breast cancer, and career ambition on her Instagram (@coopskisses). She was also been published in Wildfire Magazine, a magazine for young survivors with a focus on content written by young survivors. Danielle is a native Oregonian and graduated from Portland State University with a degree in Business. She now works for Daimler Trucks North America as a project manager and loves all things related to Heavy Duty Trucking. When she isn't working, making resin bookmarks & book holders for her small business, Hold It There (hold-it-there.com), or reading fantasy fiction, she is spending time with her son and husband.

Connect with Danielle:
Instagram: @coopskisses

WAVE AFTER WAVE OF PINK

How Diamonds are Formed
Tana Haigler

I am a mom of three boys, and I'm a breast cancer survivor. I want to tell my story to encourage other women in their fight. Having breast cancer is hard, and even with support, you can still feel alone.

About 15 years ago when I was doing my breast exam, I discovered a green discharge, I noticed it mostly coming from my left side, but it was seeping from the right side as well. I went to my gynecologist, actually, I went to her many times over the years and she would blow off my concerns saying it was just lumpy breasts.

Fast forward to three years ago. I felt a lump the size of a small pea in my left breast, right underneath the nipple. My first thought was "well that's kind of weird". My boyfriend Shawn works in the medical field, and when I told him, he said, "Oh no, you really need to get that checked." I told him I already had a feeling I knew what it was. What I wanted to do was ignore it, but I called my gynecologist and said, hey we need to do a more thorough exam. On the day of my appointment, my regular gynecologist was out of the office and I ended up seeing her PA (Physician's Assistant). She assured me she thought it was nothing to worry about, but at the same time, she advised me to have a mammogram. So, I went in for a mammogram and it was nothing, the results came back negative. About a week later, I had this flash of a fever come over me. I know it was God saying, "check your armpits". So, I checked under my arm and immediately I felt a peanut-sized lump in my armpit. And at that moment, I just knew—I had breast cancer.

I called my family doctor, and I said, "Hey, I found a lump in my armpit, I need to see you". He had an opening a couple of days later and I went in for an exam. He had me hold both arms out as he checked my armpit. I remember the look on his face—he was kind of scared. I told him he should not play poker; it was easy to read the worry on his face. He said I needed to have an ultrasound right away. He asked about my recent mammogram, and I told him it had come back negative.

My ultrasound and biopsy were done on a Thursday. The following Monday, I got a call at work and they told me that I had IDC (Invasive Ductal Carcinoma). I knew what carcinoma was—I said WHAT? So, I have cancer? He said yes, and I'm going to set you up with a medical team who is going to take really good care of you. I couldn't comprehend what he was saying, I got stuck on the word carcinoma, so I just said okay. He said he would make sure the team was in place and they would start calling me to get everything set up. I hung up the phone, ran to my coworker, and told him I have breast cancer. He hugged me. I think I was in shock; I was kind of crying but kind of not crying. I went back to my office and called Shawn and told him. I don't know what I was thinking, but I didn't consider it to be a big deal at the time. I thought it was my cancer, and I would just deal with it. I suppose I was in denial. The next call was to my sister Cindy, my best friend and biggest cheerleader. She said, "oh my gosh! You have to let me know about every appointment and what's going on". She was right there beside me from that moment on, through everything.

I knew about the cancer for about a week before I told my three boys. They are just amazing young men who have been so supportive and loving. They each dealt with my diagnosis in different ways. It was really hard for me to see the look on their faces, they were scared but they didn't want to show it. Just like me, I was scared but I wouldn't allow myself to show how I felt and I didn't cry a lot where anyone could see. I cried in silence and in private so they wouldn't be scared. I just wanted them to be okay.

I was not in a very healthy place. I didn't know what to do with myself. I was calling in sick all the time to work because mentally I was just not ok. I was fighting to be happy and make everybody else around me feel good because they were all scared. I hated it, but I think it was worse for everybody else around me. I had developed the mindset of "I'll get over it. I don't want to talk about it". I never allowed myself to ask, "why me?" Instead, I would say thank you. Thank you that it's not my children. Thank you for it not happening to my sister. My sister used to say if I could, I would take this from you. I would laugh and tell her you're not strong enough, you can't handle this.

They implanted markers when I had my biopsy. The markers were tiny pieces of titanium that would show in the scans where the cancer was in my breasts. I was officially diagnosed with HER2 triple-positive IDC Invasive Ductal Carcinoma. Since it had traveled into my lymph nodes, it was considered metastatic. When I went to my first few doctor appointments, I shut down. I felt like I was listening to the teacher on the Charlie Brown cartoons, I would hear a whole lot of "Wah wah woh wah wah" and not what the doctor was saying. Shawn and my sister, Cindy went to my appointments with me and I counted on them to listen and keep me informed. I did have questions. I wanted to know if I was going to lose my hair and if I could still have wine. The doctor said yes and yes. I was so pissed I was going to lose my hair! I remember I cried for about 10 minutes because I worked so hard to grow my hair. But then I refocused on what was going to be the best plan for me. After the initial visit, we hit the ground running.

Within the next week, I had my chemo port placed and I got a call that they wanted to start my treatment on July 4th. It's not how I wanted to remember my Fourth of July, so I asked to have it moved to July 10th. The chemo port was implanted on my right side, just below my collarbone. It sat right where the seat belt goes across your body. Right where your bra strap lays. You could see the outline of it under my skin. I noticed people looking at the lump under my skin out of curiosity. I went to my first treatment and it was really painful. The chemo port is placed under your skin, and each time you go in, they insert a needle through your skin into the port, and then the needle would lock into the back of the port. After the first three treatments, I told my doctor I needed some numbing medicine. I learned early on to be my own advocate. I had to speak up and "fire" one of the technicians because I thought she was too rough, I don't know—maybe she was just too new. I needed someone to be gentle and take better care of me. The next tech was better, and she was there every time I went in after that. She came to know I didn't want to take a deep breath or count to ten. I didn't want to watch when she put the needle in, I just wanted to look the other way while she took care of me. I was lucky, I never threw up or got sick. I was nauseous a couple of times, and everything tasted too salty. Other than the pain from accessing the port, it was probably what I hated the most about the treatment.

After my third week of treatment, I started to have chemo brain. I felt like I was in a fog. I would forget anything I was told almost immediately. I would say "oh my gosh I don't even know what you said, could you please repeat yourself?" I couldn't remember people's names. It was hard to remember things for work. If I set something down, I would forget where I put it. I couldn't tell stories or remember dates. It would take me a long time to pick a gallon of bleach because there were too many choices. My brain would go into overload. It felt almost like a short-term electrical shock. If I had something important coming up, I was afraid I would forget. I started writing things down, or I would tell my children or my sister so they could help remind me. My sister would always call me the night before and remind me I had an appointment the next morning. When she lived near me, she would come to pick me up and take me to my appointments. She lived in Bend until about halfway through my treatments and then she and her husband moved to Arizona. It broke her heart because she wasn't there when I had my surgery. It was so scary to see the nurse put on a face shield and a full-body chemical protective gown just before hooking me up to my bright orange chemo. I would watch it go down the tube until it went into my port. I felt radioactive. I used to tell my sister I felt like I was glowing.

After exactly 14 days of treatments, I started losing my hair. I woke up one morning, and I had hair on my pillow. I cried and cried. I was a little freaked out and called my sister. She loaned me a pair of shears that one of her girlfriends had used to shave her head. After a couple of days, I was ready and Shawn helped me shave my head. A bottle of wine later, and it was done. I couldn't look at myself right away, it was hard. Lots of hats and scarves helped me to cope. Everywhere I went, I felt like a walking billboard. You can wear a beanie, but you still have that cancer look. People can still tell. My eyebrows fell out and then I lost my eyelashes. It felt like an overnight change to everything familiar about my body. I told my doctor I didn't want to know the side effects of the medications. Because, if I know the side effects, it's going to get in my head, and then it's all I think about. We agreed I'd let him know when something happened to me or if I felt weird or different. Not knowing didn't spare me from the side effects, it helped me not to focus on them. The side effects of the Taxol made my face feel funny. My doctor switched me to a vaccine, and one of the side effects of the vaccine is losing your fingernails. The nails turn red and then black at the base before they lift off. I lost three fingernails. The medication also threw me into menopause at age 46. I have hot flashes and I can't control my body temperature. I'm hot, I'm cold. One arm might be freezing cold and the other arm is on fire. There isn't any rhyme or reason to it. I went through forty rounds of chemo and twenty-five straight days of radiation. Treatment becomes your life. First, you go every week, and then every single day to the hospital. It's a routine you get used to, and it becomes your life. And when it ends, you think well now what? They tell you that you're done, and if you have any further symptoms to let them know. What does that even mean? By now you feel like you are so in touch with everything happening with your body, but then you think how do I know if it's something I should even call about? The radiation burned the skin under my armpit and turned it black. The piece that was burned was about as big as my hand. I ended up in the Emergency Room to have it cut off because I was afraid, I was going to snag it on something. Thankfully it has healed now, and you can't even tell the difference.

After my chemo and radiation treatments, I had a double mastectomy and the removal of seven lymph nodes (axillary node dissection). Shawn and my oldest brother were there for me when I had surgery. Shawn's ex-wife, her mom, and daughter were also there. His ex-wife's sister had gone through brain cancer and almost died, so they understood what we were going through and were very supportive. We all prayed together before I went into surgery. I'm so thankful they were there. I think about how strange it was to have my boyfriend's ex-wife supporting me, but I guess you just have to pick and choose your battles. This fight is not one to fight alone, and they came to stand and fight with me. They were also huge supporters at the fundraiser that was held for me. We are good friends to this day.

Remember diamonds are created under pressure so hold on, it will be your time to shine soon. — Sope Agbelusi

I love this quote about how diamonds are formed under pressure. A diamond has to go through immense pressure to become a beautiful gem. Diamonds start out as an ugly rock that is crushed and changed by tremendous pressure. The diamond is cut and created into a beautiful sparkling jewel. It encourages me and has become a metaphor for me; keep your head up and know this doesn't define you. You are not cancer. I say I'm a survivor of chemo.

Maybe cancer would have eventually killed me, but it's the chemo that is toxic.

My mastectomy and reconstruction were a 10-hour surgery. My cancer surgeon completely removed my breasts, all of my breast tissue, and the affected lymph nodes under my arm. Once that was complete, my plastic surgeon came in to place the tissue expanders. About a week after surgery, they begin to inject saline fluid into a port in the expanders. The expanders are small pouches used to stretch the tissue and muscle to prepare you for implants. It takes several weeks until the expanders have created enough space for the implants. The implant surgery was about 4 or 5 weeks after the expanders were placed. They remove the expanders and replace them with the implants. It was a painful process. After my surgery, I had drain tubes coming out of my side. So not only was I bald, I felt like a science project. I don't know how else to explain it. I would tell myself this is just a momentary thing; this is not forever.

At one of my post-surgery appointments, my plastic surgeon noticed a scab where the drain tube was coming out. He scolded me, as if I hadn't been showering and cleaning the wound. But I had been. Suddenly he just picked it off, and boy did it hurt! I grabbed his arm without even thinking, it hurt so bad. I think he was pretty surprised. He told me to let go of his jacket. I told him well then, don't do that again within arm's reach of me — because if I can reach you, I'm going to grab you.

I lost my job. I was struggling to pay my bills. I was prescribed Neulasta steroid shots. They are $12,000 each. There was a mix-up in the billing at the pharmacy and I found out another medication I have to take is $323 per pill without insurance. When I saw that, I felt like I was having a heart attack. I called the pharmacy and found out someone entered the wrong number for my insurance. But with insurance, it was still over $50 per pill. How do they sleep at night? It's insane. It breaks my heart and makes me angry that people can't afford their medication. An advocate at the St. Charles Cancer Center helped me to sign up for a program to help with non-medical living expenses, such as transportation, lodging, utility bills, and rent. The program provides you with food cards to buy groceries, and gas cards to help you get to your appointments. They even helped with my electric bill. The medical bills were staggering. I was looking at over $400,000 for my treatment. The advocate helped me sign up for a medical assistance program. I was sponsored by the hospital and they ended up paying for all my bills. I cried when I got the letter, there was just no way I could afford it. None whatsoever. It was a true blessing.

I have to go back in for another surgery because my left implant is encapsulated, it's as hard as a baseball. My choices are getting the implant removed and going flat or having fat, skin, and muscle from my back or my stomach used to reconstruct. I haven't made that decision yet; I've just been living with using pads to make my breasts look even. It's a struggle to see your body go through these complications after everything else that's happened. Sometimes I wonder if I made the right choice by getting the implants. Should I Have gone flat? They found cancer on both sides, so I had no other choice than a double mastectomy. I don't know if the reason I wanted the implants was that I was vain, or because they were there my whole life and I guess I was just used to them.

After implant surgery, you no longer have nipples. Honestly, it was weird to look in the mirror and not recognize my own body. After surgery, some people have their nipples tattooed, but I wasn't a candidate because my skin was too thin. I started to research prosthetic nipples. I wanted something inexpensive, realistic looking, and made in America. I found a company called Naturally Impressive. It was started by a nurse who is a breast cancer survivor and her husband. I called and spoke with her personally to learn more. We shared our stories and I fell in love with her and her mission. I bought three sets from her. They make me feel incredible and whole.

My advocate at the cancer center told me about the Pink Sistas Retreats. My first thought was oh great I don't want to go sit in a circle and talk to a group of women about my breast cancer or feel like I'm about to stand and speak at an AA meeting. "My name is Tana, and I have cancer..." I didn't like to go to events because everyone wanted to share their opinion. You should try this naturopathic method. You should smoke some CBD. You should use these oils on your body. Have you thought about doing a cleanse? I just wanted to turn off all the unsolicited advice. So, I may have had a little bit of an attitude when I showed up for the retreat. It was like okay I'm here—I guess I'm supposed to do this now because I have cancer. I'll just be another one of those statistical women who goes to retreats or attends groups and bares my soul, but it wasn't like that at all. When I went to the retreat, I was struggling with chemo brain. I would start to say something and then forget what I was talking about. At one time or another, I feel like all of us would forget what we were saying and have to stop. But the wonderful thing about being there with people who understood was that if someone's brain was not engaging, another person would just jump in. It was such a wonderful thing. I feel I have a good sense of what other women are feeling or going through. If they are feeling alone, I want to encourage them and take some of the fear away. Let them know how they are feeling is not weird or strange. I probably talk too much about private things like what your body goes through, but I throw it out there because there might be a chance it will help someone who is struggling with the silence of this horrible illness. Honestly, the retreat was amazing. I was just so rejuvenated and full of life and on fire when I got home. I think we talked to one another just one time about our cancer journey, and the rest of the time we relaxed. We went out on the boat, and some of the ladies learned how to paddleboard. At that point in my recovery, I wasn't strong enough to learn paddle boarding. Plus, I'm not a good swimmer, so I generally pass on the water stuff. But it didn't matter, we bonded. We had a weekend away from cancer. I'm so thankful for Pink Sistas and how Deb supports women with breast cancer. I wish I had other words to express what it does for you, instead of just saying it is a group of women who have something in common. It is so much more than that. We came from different walks of life, we had different personalities. We could relate to each other, and we knew what each other was going through without really having to say too many words about it.

There is pain in life that uses you and there is pain that you can use.
— Darlene Snell

All of the things you have to deal with, and then when you're finally healing, you find out your new boob is encapsulated. Why can't it just be easy? Why can't you go through it, get through it, and then just be done with it? And then be able to say okay that's all behind me. I don't know but I guess God's not done with me. I don't know how else to explain it. I think I went through this so I could encourage other women and help them fight. It's hard to feel alone, no one can tell you how to feel because cancer is unique for everyone, and everybody deals with it differently. I chose to use my pain, this journey has changed me for the better, forever!

Tana Haigler

My name is Tana. I'm a mother of 3 amazing young men, a sister, an aunt, a friend, but most of all, a child of God. He carries me through all the trials and triumphs in my life. I believe in being positive and having compassion for others. I hope that you find peace and know that you're not alone. This journey is yours, share what you want and be a light, because you never know who needs to hear you care.

Connect with Tana:
Facebook: Tana Haigler Powell

WAVE AFTER WAVE OF PINK

Finding Out I Had Cancer

Andrea Davis

The phone rang at about 6:00 pm. I had been expecting the call.

"Hi, is this Andrea? This is Doctor Germino. I performed your biopsy the other day. I just received the results."

I stopped breathing.

"We did biopsies of two areas and got similar findings. What we found is invasive ductal carcinoma. That means the cancer is malignant. We have reason to believe it will be responsive to treatment." Her voice sounded precise, but I also detected caring and a note of concern about me. "I know this is a lot of information."

I took a deep breath. And then I started writing down what she was saying in a notebook I had set out specifically for this phone call. "That's okay. I'm okay," I said. "I want you to tell me everything you can. I'm writing it down."

"We think there may be two separate masses," Doctor Germino continued. "There is one mass located at about six o'clock. It appears to be about 12 millimeters, which is 1.2 centimeters. There's another mass at about nine o'clock. That one appears to be 5.2 centimeters."

5.2 centimeters. Jesus. The thing was huge!

"Both tumors are responsive to estrogen. They are also positive for something called the HER2 protein. There are specific treatments for HER2+ tumors that we expect will be effective. The lymph node we biopsied also shows cancer."

Ouch.

"You'll be referred to a surgeon and an oncologist. They'll want to shrink the tumor first with chemotherapy. You'll go through a process called staging where they look for tumors elsewhere in the body."

Elsewhere in the body? I quickly postponed my horrified thoughts. One step at a time, Andrea.

"There are two nurse navigators who are there to guide patients through the process. One of them will give you a call, probably tomorrow.

"I know this may sound crazy to say, but if I had a big breast tumor, I'd want it to be a HER2+ tumor. There have been so many great advances in how HER2+ tumors are treated." She paused for a moment. "Do you have any questions about anything?"

I thought for a moment. "How do I know what I'm supposed to do next?"

"The nurse navigator who calls you will let you know what to do," Doctor Germino told me. "My guess is that you'll be meeting with the oncologist first, but I don't know for sure. But she'll go over all of that with you. That's her job, to guide you through the process."

We talked for a few more minutes. Doctor Germino made sure I had no more questions for the time being. Then we said goodnight, and I hung up the phone.

I sat there.

I had breast cancer, the tumor was big and there was cancer in at least one lymph node. They would be doing scans to see if I had tumors in other parts of my body.

I felt a surge of adrenaline and a tingle of fear. But I also felt a sense of calm. This was my reality. There was no disputing it. I was going to do whatever I needed to do about this, one thing at a time.

For right now, I needed to call John and let him know. John We were both passionate nature lovers and loved hiking and backpacking together.

At the time, I wanted more than anything to make a living as a farmer. We purchased our farm property together in 1998.

By 2015, our relationship was falling apart. We were hosting a constant stream of live-in farm volunteers through the World Wide Opportunities on Organic Farms (WWOOF) program. John was distancing himself from the farm more and more, while I worked harder and harder.

Things came to a head in 2015, and I told him I would leave unless he would go to counseling with me. Preparing to tell him this—and possibly to leave my life on the farm— had been excruciating. But it turned out to be worth it. We went to counseling every week for six months, and we both started to see we needed to make some big changes in how we handled ourselves and our relationship.

Now, I knew John would be there for me no matter what I was going to have to go through. I was so grateful for all that work we had done less than two years earlier. I felt certain that we could travel this road together, no matter what happened.

But right now, John was gone. Our neighbor across the river had invited us on a skiing and mountain biking vacation in Central Oregon. I hadn't gone because I needed to get the biopsy done and find out the results.

I had encouraged him to go. I knew being with people, being away from home, and getting a lot of exercise would help him.

I dialed his cell phone number. "Hi, Puppy."

"Hi, sweetheart. Did you find anything out yet?" He sounded worried.

"Yeah, I just got a phone call from the doctor who did the biopsy. She said I have breast cancer. I have two tumors. One is about 1.2 centimeters and one is 5.2 centimeters. And there's cancer in the lymph node she biopsied too."

He was silent for a moment. "So, she just called you? You just found out?"

"Yup. I just found out. I'm glad she called me tonight, so I didn't have to wait any longer."

"That was really nice that she called you tonight."

"It is. I know." I paused. "I'm sorry, John. I know this is really hard for you, too."

"We'll get through this, Andrea. We're going to do what we need to do, and we'll get through this," he said in his calm, steady way.

"I know we are, Puppy. I know we are," I told him quietly, tears starting to run down my nose.

Tough Times

I won't pretend it was a bed of roses. About six days after my first chemo treatment, nausea and diarrhea set in, to the point where I doubted my ability to make it through the next five chemo treatments.

A local acupuncturist who specializes in helping cancer patients gave me acupuncture designed to help my digestive system, and it seemed to help. I decided to have acupuncture once a week for the first two weeks after every chemo infusion, and I think it made a huge difference. The acupuncturist also advised me to take probiotics, fish oil, and other supplements that I think helped me a great deal while I was on chemo.

A little over a month into chemo, I was hospitalized for a blood infection that apparently started when my chemo port was placed. For the next four days, I was given intravenous vancomycin, an extremely strong antibiotic designed to kill MRSA.

The vancomycin gave me painful phlebitis and didn't get rid of the infection. The doctors finally decided to try a different antibiotic. After a couple of days, my blood work started showing a decrease in the number of staphylococcus bacteria.

On my eighth morning there, my nurse was jubilant. She told me my blood cultures had finally been negative for forty-eight hours, which meant I got to go home.

A nurse at the Infusion Center trained me and John in how to administer the IVs at home and gave me a week's worth of supplies, which we had to refill four times.

Being on chemo and heavy-duty antibiotics at the same time was definitely no joyride for my stomach. But with the help of acupuncture treatments, smaller, more frequent meals, Britain's Got Talent videos, and probiotic supplements that I carefully took right in the middle of the eight hours between each antibiotic infusion, I made it through. "Yay! It's only chemo from now on!" I chortled on my last day of antibiotic infusions.

Shock and Devastation

One of my most shocking moments came while John and I were meeting with a breast surgeon in Portland.

"Because there appear to be two tumors," she told me, "We recommend a mastectomy. And that's because there could be other cancer cells between the tumors. If we do a lumpectomy, we might not get them all."

My mouth was suddenly dry, and my heart dropped into my shoes. "I thought I would be able to have a lumpectomy," I managed to say. "Not a mastectomy."

"We always recommend a mastectomy in your situation," Doctor Naik reiterated.

After she left, I said quietly and shakily to John, "I didn't think I would have to have a mastectomy." John reached out and enfolded me in his arms.

"I don't want to have a mastectomy," I sobbed. "God damn it! I'll do it if I have to, but I don't want to have to do it! I do **not** want to have to do it!"

"Oh, Bunny," John said softly and held me tighter while I cried.

The Beauty of Caring

Family, friends, and neighbors came to my aid in profound, surprising ways. John's sister Lisa was on sabbatical that year and made it clear that she wanted to help in any way she could. She gave me rides home from chemotherapy and other treatments, took me shopping, and sometimes made food for me and John. Lisa and I had many long conversations in the car, getting to know each other at a depth that our busy lives had, up until now, prevented.

My friend Lorraine came to most of my chemotherapy treatments with rune cards and book passages she read to me. My neighbor Sarah, whose mom died of ovarian cancer just a few years earlier, came over with a soft pink and white blanket. She picked out the fabric, especially for me, and had sewn on the pink edging.

Various people made food for us when I was first home from the hospital after the blood infection, and again after my mastectomy surgery in June.

Friends from a close-knit neighborhood in south Corvallis—many of whom I had hardly seen since I stopped running my booth at the Corvallis farmers market nearly a year earlier—pruned most of our 400 blueberry bushes while I was home recovering, a time-consuming act of love which brought me to tears.

In the two decades before getting diagnosed, I had often been so busy working on our small farm, making jams to sell, running my weekly farmers market booth, and hosting hundreds of live-in farm volunteers, that I had not made a lot of room for friendships. And certainly not for anyone in need. I thought of lasting social connections as somewhat frivolous "extras" that could be dispensed with when I just didn't have time for them.

Being the recipient of so much love and care woke me up to a profound truth: caring about other humans is not just a nice "extra" thing to do. The care that I received was essential. I wanted to make more room in my life to care for others.

Finding A Support Group

Chemotherapy ended in mid-April. We scheduled my mastectomy surgery for mid-June. I was grief-stricken about having to lose my breast. But my surgeon, Doctor Faddis, made it clear to me and John that he recommended a mastectomy. I had two tumors, and one of them was over five centimeters. Doctor Faddis pointed out that if he performed a lumpectomy, not only would it be difficult to make sure he was getting rid of all the cancer, but there wouldn't be a whole lot left of my breast.

I trusted Doctor Faddis. He was extremely respectful and thorough with us, without being at all pushy. I knew he did these surgeries all the time. I didn't like his recommendation, but I would follow it.

I started looking for women who could understand what I was going through and tell me about their experiences. I contacted Project H.E.R. in Corvallis. Project H.E.R. provides awareness, education, and support for all women— from the time of a breast cancer diagnosis through survivorship. I spoke with Parker Cochran who asked about the details of my diagnosis and treatment and assigned me a mentor named Anne.

Anne talked at length on the phone with me. She had been diagnosed about five years earlier. Her diagnosis was quite similar to mine: her tumor was also large and HER2+. Her biopsy had also shown cancer in a lymph node. And she also had a mastectomy.

Anne made it clear that she was there to support me in any way she could. And she invited me to the Young Adult Cancer Survivors group (YACS) that met—and continues to meet—monthly at the Cancer Center where I was getting treated.

"Young adult? Are you sure that's okay? I'm fifty-four," I told her.

"You're so active," she told me. "I think you should come."

Still almost completely bald from chemotherapy, still wearing a headscarf, I drove out to the Cancer Center to attend the group for the first time in May. There were eight or nine other breast cancer survivors there who had already been through treatment. Many of them had had mastectomies.

I brought out my list of questions. How much had their range of motion been impacted by the surgery? How long did it take them to recover? If they had reconstruction, how was their experience of it? If they didn't have it, why not? Were they happy with their choice?

They answered my questions and then some. I got to share my fear and my grief. I felt held and understood by women who'd been through it. They focused on my situation for most of the meeting.

Pink Sistas

The following year, after I'd been through a mastectomy and radiation, after my last Herceptin treatment, and after my hair had grown back enough for me to have it cut for the first time, Anne emailed all the members of the YACS group to let us know that she wanted to organize a group of us to go on a retreat together in August.

Anne told us Deb Hart, who ran a nonprofit called Pink Sistas, organized the retreats. We would get to stay at Deb's floating home in the Columbia River for two nights. They would provide all our food, and we'd make jewelry and do yoga and other activities. What's more, the retreat was free. Any woman who'd been diagnosed with breast cancer was eligible to go to one Pink Sistas retreat in her lifetime.

I knew right away I wanted to go. It was tricky figuring out a date that worked for everyone. We settled on a weekend in August. Right in the middle of blueberry U-pick season on our farm.

We have just a half-acre of U-pick—not big enough to pay employees. A few years ago, I never would have left on an August weekend. But things had changed. I had changed. I found a way to make it work.

Deb welcomed us warmly and cooked for us. The first night, we shared our stories, and she told us hers. "But from now on," she said afterward, "We're not going to talk about cancer."

The next day, a yoga instructor came and led us in a class for over an hour. A couple of instructors came and showed us how to paddleboard. We spent time relaxing. A jewelry maker came and guided us each in making two pieces of jewelry. We all went for a walk along the docks together. Deb took us for a boat ride. I felt exhilarated and satisfied from spending so much time outdoors and so much time connecting with the other women.

On the last morning of the retreat, I woke up early, picked up my journal and pen, and padded up to the top deck. The mist was rising softly off the Columbia River. I saw an egret and some ospreys. My heart was full.

"I don't want to spend so much time worrying about me anymore," I wrote. "I want to focus more on giving."

Watching the water and the birds, I thought silently, "Please show me the best way for me to give."

Andrea Davis

Andrea Davis holds a certificate in Advanced Life Skills Coaching from Stonebrook Associated Colleges.

Andrea now offers wellness coaching to cancer patients, helping them find energy, joy, and better health through research- backed strategies.

She'll be co-leading a two-day retreat for metastatic breast cancer patients with Deb Hart of Pink Sistas in November 2020.

Andrea was diagnosed with Stage 3 triple-positive breast cancer in December 2017 and had chemotherapy, a mastectomy, and radiation.

She also used multiple holistic strategies to fight her cancer, including diet, exercise, supplements, meditation, and the priceless support of many family members and friends.

There's no evidence of cancer in her body today.

Andrea loves gardening, walking and hiking, making music and singing, and spending time with friends and family.

She grows half an acre of U-pick blueberries on her organic farm in Kings Valley, a rural community in western Oregon where she's lived for more than 21 years with her partner, John Madsen.

Connect with Andrea
Email: andrea@andreadaviscancercoaching.com
Website: https://andreadaviscancercoaching.com

WAVE AFTER WAVE OF PINK

Saving Grace

Jana Hill

Although the day when I found a lump in my right breast is unremembered.... finding it was a total accident. Only because it was hard, small, and poked out slightly from beneath my skin. It felt just like a little rock. I was working as a yoga instructor at two local gyms and a skincare specialist at Nordstrom. It was sometime during the summer of 2015.

It's weird, I had a fear, almost an inkling that I might get breast cancer in my life. The thought popped into my head one-day several years ago and it stayed although I didn't think about it too often. When I found the lump, I knew it was different. It was strange. I wanted to get it checked out but I didn't have health insurance. Employee benefits at my job had a window of time allotted for signing up for health insurance and I had missed it. I had to wait until the end of the year. Once that time came and I was finally able to go to the doctor, it was January of 2016. Around 6 months after initially finding the lump.

I was on my lunch break at work when I got a phone call from my nurse. This was after having a breast checkup, a mammogram, an ultrasound, and finally a biopsy. I was somewhat stunned to hear that I had breast cancer. Stage 1 invasive ductal carcinoma. Estrogen positive. I was scared and fearful. I started sobbing on the phone as my life started to flip upside down. I was consoled by coworkers but I knew I had to leave at that moment. I didn't' go back to work. I went home and thought about how I was going to tell my parents, friends, and family. I also canceled a trip to California that was coming up in just a few days. This would be the beginning of a long road, a journey, something I had no idea how to handle. My life would solely be to start focusing on moving forward with my battle with breast cancer. I had no idea how much my life would change over the next year.

After telling my family, I told a few close friends. One of them told me about an amazing woman named Deb Hart that runs a nonprofit for breast cancer fighters and survivors called "Pink Sistas". My friend told me Deb was a breast cancer survivor and had written a book. My friend had a copy and let me borrow it. Not too long after that, I opened the book to read it and I couldn't put it down. It was well written and very interesting. It was also emotional. My friend told Deb about me and soon Deb and I were in touch. Meeting her was wonderful and I got to learn all about the retreats she held through her nonprofit "Pink Sistas". I was so interested in attending but wanted to wait until after my treatment.

The first week after I was diagnosed was full of many doctors' appointments. Lab work, testing, MRI, surgery scheduling, and meeting my oncologist. You name it, my week was packed nonstop. After meeting with everyone, I decided to go with a double mastectomy. I would undergo chemotherapy after my surgery but no radiation. The doctor said that since I was having a double mastectomy, AND that my cancer was only stage 1, I wouldn't need radiation. I would have only four chemo treatments, but that is because I was going to be given the harshest form of chemotherapy there was. Just like with most things in my life, I grabbed this situation by the horns and did what I needed to do to get through it. I went nonstop and didn't look back. I followed all of my doctors' orders, changed my diet, researched heavily, and immersed myself in my fitness routine.

The biggest change I saw in myself from this was my attitude towards life and the way I lived. I let go of fear. Fear of not going after what I wanted to achieve, fear of what others thought of me, and fear of the future. Once I let go of fear and replaced it with faith, my life changed so much. If only I could have lived this way before. It took getting breast cancer for me to live my life the way I truly wanted to. I wanted to help others do the same. I also wanted to inspire others in any way that I could. I hoped I would continue living this way even after my battle was over and my life went back to normal.

After undergoing my double mastectomy, I had a downfall. I wasn't healing well at all. I came home from the hospital and didn't give myself enough downtime. I was using my arms too much and moving around too soon. I ended up getting a blood clot in my right breast and had to undergo emergency surgery after seeing my doctor. It was one of the hardest things I had to deal with in all of this. It took me so long to heal. I would go in for my checkups and my doctor would say, 'you're just not healing well". Or he would say it's taking longer than usual for you to heal. It was frustrating because, at that point, I was doing everything I was supposed to do. I was taking really good care of myself. It felt like an eternity as I lay in bed every day trying to heal. A friend of mine told me to be patient and love your body, it's working hard for you right now. Those words helped me a lot.

Once I was feeling better, I started tissue expansion every two weeks to prepare my body for breast implants. Once I was healed enough, I started working out again gently. I eased into it and continued teaching my yoga classes!

Yoga and fitness were my saving grace. Instead of staying home and being depressed, I got myself to the gym and worked out when I could. I was on a pretty regular schedule and feeling really good. I was getting in even better shape than I was before I was diagnosed with breast cancer. I was starting to inspire people around me which felt amazing. That's when I started thinking about working as a personal trainer. It's something I had thought about for years but never pursued. I kept it in the forefront of my mind.

Not soon after that, I began my chemotherapy treatments. They were scheduled every 3 weeks. It was tuff because I had to take the medication with it, give myself shots, and continue tissue expansion. Dealing with the side effects of the chemo. I prevailed and stayed strong with my workouts and teaching yoga classes. There were so many days when I felt so horrible, I didn't think I could bare teaching my yoga class or going to the gym, or even getting out of bed but most of the time I FORCED myself. It wasn't easy, but by the time I was done, I felt so much better. Wow, I had proven to myself that I was stronger both mentally and physically than I thought. If I could do this, so could others that are going through the same thing.

I eventually lost all my hair and started wearing scarves and got a really cute wig. During this time, I was invited to be a part of the "Pink Sistas" calendar that would be published for the following year! The photoshoot was a lot of fun! I took pictures on a paddleboard. It was my first time on one and I was so nervous! We also went out on a huge boat and got a lot of really fun pictures! We also had some get-togethers after the shoot with all the other ladies. As I was nearing the end of my chemo treatments I seriously started considering working as a personal trainer. I began my studies and trained at a fitness facility in Happy Valley. I loved it there and it felt like family. The environment was awesome and I felt like I was in my element. By the end of the summer of 2016, I was working as a personal trainer and continued working as a yoga instructor. I was happy. My story not only inspired others but motivated them as well. It was around this same time I was done with my chemotherapy and tissue expansions. I was preparing for my breast implant surgery. That took place at the end of September. I got myself really strong before surgery and allowed myself plenty of time for healing. I had built up a clientele and started growing my social media platforms. It's always hard taking breaks from life when you have to have surgery but I allowed myself that time to relax and not be too hard on myself. I knew I could pick back up where I left off and If I let go of that fear and held onto my faith, everything would be ok.

Once I was healed, I felt like it was the perfect time to go on a "Pink Sistas" Retreat. It was a weekend retreat in Pine Hollow, Oregon. It was such a great time. Meeting the other ladies was cool and I liked connecting with women who had been through the same or similar situations as myself. Everyone was great and Deb was the best hostess! The food was incredible too! We did a lot of different things like jewelry making, hiking, and fellowship. I even led the ladies in a yoga class! Pine Hollow was beautiful and relaxing. I felt a lot of gratitude that weekend.

After I got home, I prepared for another surgery. I needed another breast augmentation as the first one left my breasts very uneven and different sizes. To make my breasts more even, this surgery consisted of some fat grafting. I also elected to have nipple reconstruction. I've been a little bit of a perfectionist my whole life so it was hard not having beautiful breasts... But after going through this experience, I humbled myself and accepted that my breasts would never be perfect. Getting and dealing with breast cancer has changed my life for the best. Going forward, I just want to live my life with love and be the healthiest, happiest version of myself!

The last and hopefully final surgery I had was a full hysterectomy. That was a really hard surgery for me... It took a while to feel "normal" again but I tried my best. I took part in several more Pink Sistas events since then. About a year after my hysterectomy, I got to be in a fundraiser for Pink Sistas at a beautiful restaurant. My daughter and I did it together and my son came along. We had a yummy lunch after the fashion show and it was all for a good cause!

I also attended the Pink Sistas' biggest fundraiser of the year a couple of years ago in Troutdale. There was a silent auction, live band, food, and fun! I was so excited to be able to finally attend that one as it was my first time!

Lastly, this past summer I attended a day retreat with the Pink Sistas on their houseboat out on the river. We went boating, paddle boarding, and kayaking out by the boathouses where there weren't many currents. I was so proud of myself because I was able to stand up on the paddleboard! It was so much fun being on the water and meeting new friends. I'll always be grateful for my amazing experiences with Pink Sistas. There always seems to be something positive you can take from negative situations. For me, it was my experiences with Pink Sistas and making new friends as well as growing friendships I already had.

Jana Hill

Jana Hill is a mother, yoga instructor, and aesthetician.

Her children mean everything to her and she loves living life to its fullest.

Jana's hobbies include reading, working out, and photography.

Her favorite way to enjoy her time is with her family.

Jana received her diagnosis of Stage 1 breast cancer at age thirty-seven.

Jana was working as a personal trainer and yoga instructor at the time. Keeping active in her health and fitness was her saving grace. It helped her to deal with the emotional and physical side effects of chemotherapy and fighting cancer.

Jana is nearing her five-year mark of being cancer-free.

Connect with Jana
Email: Janaleehill@gmail.com
Instagram: @janaleefitness
Instagram: @beautybyjanalee

WAVE AFTER WAVE OF PINK

Roller Coaster
Delo Fercho

I went to the doctor for a routine mammogram. While I was still at the hospital getting the mammogram, the technician came to me and said she needed to have the doctor read my mammogram. The doctor asked me if I would go over to another hospital and have a biopsy that day.

My husband Randy and I have been together for fifteen years. He was working that day, and he wasn't able to go with me. My dad came from Kelso, Washington, to meet me at the hospital in Portland, Oregon, for the biopsy.

After they take a biopsy, you get to wait three days for the results. Three long days. My biopsy happened to be on a Thursday, so I didn't get the results until the following Monday. It was a very long and stressful weekend.

The Call

I clearly remember the moment the nurse navigator called and told me I had ductal carcinoma. I didn't know anything about breast cancer at the time so the only word I heard was carcinoma. What flashed through my brain was "That's cancer."

Ductal carcinoma is a common type of breast cancer that starts in cells that line the milk ducts. In most cases, surgery is the first treatment for invasive ductal carcinoma.

The nurse navigator gave me some basic information and a surgeon's name. Nurse navigators are supposed to serve as the primary contact for the patient through every step of their care using their skills and knowledge to offer patients special insight into their diagnosis and upcoming treatment journey.

Unfortunately, the call with the nurse navigator was my only contact with her. She did not offer me anything other than the name of the surgeon and never followed up with me after the call. I was left to figure out my treatment journey on my own.

When I hung up from the nurse, I texted my daughter Tiffany, my niece Tara, and my husband Randy. I said, "I need to tell you guys something." The hardest part about telling them was that I was embarrassed to say I had cancer.

They were asking me questions I had no answers for. I felt like I was on a roller coaster that I had no control over.

What's next?

I had no clue.

Removing the Cancer

At my next appointment, we scheduled a lumpectomy; it's where the surgeons go in and cut out a large part of your breast to try to remove the cancer cells.

When breast cancer is surgically removed during a surgical biopsy, lumpectomy, or mastectomy, a rim of normal tissue surrounding the tumor is also removed. This rim is called a margin. Margins help show whether or not all of the tumor was removed.

The doctor removes cells and then checks the margins around where the cells were removed. They keep removing cells until they get clear margins. Once your cells test positive for clear margins, it means no cancer cells are in the area outside of the cancer they cut out.

When I woke up from the surgery, I was really sore. I asked the surgeon, "Why am I so sore if you just did a lumpectomy?" He told me they took about a 3"x4" piece out of my breast and weren't able to get clear margins. This meant more surgery would be needed to remove any remaining cancer cells.

I had to be my own advocate, so I asked, "What do we do next?" It was disappointing to have to figure everything out by myself. The doctor told me they would need to remove the remaining breast tissue. My first thought was, what about the other side? Will I be lopsided? When I asked, he said after recovery they could do reconstruction surgery to make my breasts look the same.

Randy went to every appointment with me. He only missed one appointment, and my stepdaughter Heather went with me to that one.

I talked with the doctors about my options for reconstruction. They were very matter-of-fact and told me I could get implants at the same time as my double mastectomy surgery.

This was the appointment Heather went to with me. They showed us pictures of women with implants. It was very emotional for me; the book had pictures of women's torsos, from the belly to the neck. I thought the pictures looked like cadavers. I was scared and started crying. The pictures showed what it might look like with and without implants. I cried and cried; it was so hard to look at the pictures.

I was told the type of implants they would use were the "safest" implants, smooth like a gummy bear. I was not given the full information needed to make an informed decision. There was nothing said about what could go wrong. No one told me the lifespan of implants is only ten years, and the FDA recommends you get an MRI every year for the first three years, and once every three years after that.

I was not made aware of the disadvantages, and I opted to get immediate reconstruction with implants at the same time as my double mastectomy. I felt I needed the confidence boost after everything I had been going through and wanted to feel and look like myself. I just knew this would be my last surgery.

I didn't want any more surgeries. I think I was channeling my aunt Janet who also had breast cancer. She ended up dying; I don't know if it was breast cancer or what that she eventually died from, but I knew I didn't want to die. I opted to have both breasts removed at the same time.

We made the appointment for my double mastectomy. I had to wait four weeks until I could go in for the surgery. I was amazed when about twenty people came to the hospital to see me off to surgery. I had a conversation with my Aunt Ruth prior to surgery. I knew I needed someone to come and help take care of me afterward, and she was the only person I wanted to take care of me in my recovery. I was relieved when she said she would come and stay after the surgery.

Randy was there with me through the appointments, the surgery, and the recovery. But he still had to work, and I didn't know what to expect after a double mastectomy, I just knew that Aunt Ruth would have answers, and she did. She helped care for me and put me on a twenty-four-hour medication timetable so we would know when I should take my medicines.

And let me tell you, the pain is excruciating. You want to keep on top of the pain right after surgery and take your medication right on time, or the pain will get ahold of you. Then you have to basically start over, trying to get back on top of the pain.

About a month later, I developed large holes at the bottom of my breast where my skin was separating. I had to go back in to have one side fixed. The next week, the doctor had to go in and fix the other side.

I slept in the recliner and Randy was on the couch the whole time I was recovering. He was always there for me, through the diagnosis, appointments, surgeries, and recovery.

My dog Oliver slept on my lap and seemed to know when I needed rest. He's been so sweet and gently pats my chest when he lies with me as if he knows what I've been through. "Ah," I thought, "this will be my last surgery. I am going to get into CrossFit and really take care of myself-this is a new lease on life!" I joined a CrossFit gym and was beginning to get into really good shape. I had the opportunity to be on a dragon boat team. I was excited to join; the team is made up of about 110 other breast cancer survivors.

It felt good to compete, and it began to feel as if my life had become manageable again for the first time in a couple of years. I even decided to get tattoos of nipples on my implants and I felt whole again.

Then one day, I went to practice and couldn't get on the boat. The next thing I noticed was that I couldn't turn my head; then I couldn't swallow and started to have brain fog. The brain fog was horrible; I couldn't remember anything. I went to the doctor with my symptoms, and they did a barrage of tests. They referred me to a rheumatologist, thinking maybe I had rheumatoid arthritis. It wasn't a condition that runs in my family. My doctors put me on rounds of a steroid medication called Prednisone. It provided no relief. I absolutely didn't know what I was going to do.

Pink Sistas

At around the same time I was experiencing all of this, I got the opportunity to go on a retreat with Pink Sistas. I was so excited about the retreat, but there were stairs at the retreat. And I could barely walk.

How was I going to climb the stairs?

What would they expect of me?

I had friends who were going to the retreat the same weekend, and I really wanted to go, too.

What was amazing is when I got to the retreat, I really didn't have to do anything except keep my feet elevated. It was such a relaxing weekend. I was able to sit in the party boat and take it easy while friends played on paddleboards and with water toys. I was able to just take it easy and didn't try to do everything. No one gave me any pushback; I could participate in what I was able to participate in.

I felt really pampered, and it took my mind off of what was happening with my body.

Breast Implant Illness

After the retreat, I told my friend Mindy what I was experiencing with the brain fog and trouble walking. She asked if I had ever heard of Breast Implant Illness. In the past, I had heard of breast implants not being good for you, but I was unaware of any specifics. Breast Implant Illness (BII) is a group of autoimmune issues that can include chronic fatigue, fevers, brain fog, and joint pain.

I found a support group on Facebook and began to research Breast Implant Illness. By this time, I had about twenty-five different calls to the advice nurse and twelve different doctor appointments. No one could figure out what was wrong with me.

I had an EKG. At one point they thought I might be having a heart attack or stroke. I had an MRI, a CT scan, and a biopsy done on the fluid in my legs. Everything tested normal. The only abnormal finding was the inflammation I was experiencing. I met my insurance deductible for the year in just two months.

I asked my doctors if I could have BII. They said they didn't think it could be the implants, but I was given the choice to "explant," to have my implants removed.

After learning more about BII, I chose to have my implants removed; my explant surgery was on August 5, 2019. The moment they were removed, I started to feel better. I was able to walk again when I got home. It was exhilarating! I was ready to heal from the explant surgery and get back to living my life.

When the implants were removed, I was left with loose skin and fat. It was so frustrating, after everything I had been through, to look in the mirror. This is not how I imagined my body would ever look. I wanted to scream from the rooftops and tell everyone who would listen what implants could do to you. I contacted a local news station, and they actually did a story on me and my journey with the implants.

I'm not really a private person, and I don't keep a lot of things to myself. However, after I did the interview, as I watched it, I understood that now the world would know I got my breasts cut off. It was kind of surreal, once I thought about it afterward.

I found out about an exercise class at Oregon Health Sciences University (OHSU) put on by a team of researchers. The class is for cancer patients and their significant others to exercise together. My husband and I joined the class, and it has been a good way for me to get back into working out and back into my life.

After my implants were removed, I thought I might want to try a different type of breast reconstruction called fat grafting. In fat grafting, fat tissue is removed from other parts of your body-usually your thighs, belly, and buttocks-by liposuction. The tissue is then processed into liquid and injected into the breast area to recreate the breast.

Fat grafting would create a breast where the implants were removed, and I thought it would help me to look and feel like a woman again. I did my research on fat grafting, the advantages and disadvantages, and what could go wrong. I read that in many cases, the fat could be reabsorbed into the body and the reconstructed breast would lose volume. It could take several procedures to get results. Some of the fat injected into the breast area could die, which is called "necrosis."

Once I did my research, I chose not to get the fat grafting. There were too many disadvantages, and I wasn't willing to put my health at risk anymore. This was the first time in my journey I felt I truly had informed consent, and I got to choose what I wanted to do.

On December 23, 2019, I went under the knife one more time. I made the choice to go completely flat. It wasn't an easy decision, but it was the right decision for me. I'm now getting used to the new me. I had my doctor write me a letter that gave me the option of working out as soon as I could.

I'm recovering from my last surgery and feeling better every day. I've met many of my neighbors through a post on Facebook asking for help with walking the dog. My neighbors have been so friendly and helpful. They started a meal train for Randy and me and have been making sure Oliver goes for regular walks until I am able to walk him again.

My girls, Tiffany and Tara, along with Randy's daughter Heather, were a major part of my healing and recovery. They were there with me every step of the way. I could not have done it without them.

It's my mission to share my story. People need to know the advantages and the disadvantages of having reconstruction after breast cancer in order to make an informed decision.

You might save your own life.

Delo Fercho

Born number 4 of 6 children, Delo grew up with a great sense of frugality, she lived in several different small towns, including Gallup, New Mexico and finally graduating in Longview, a small town in Washington.

Delo was bitten by the entrepreneurial bug at an early age when she saw she could make a lot more money working for herself. While her friends were off searching for jobs, she was out starting businesses.

Delo married the love of her life Randy in 2007 and they reside in Oregon with their Llaso/Maltese mix Oliver. They are empty-nesters, with grown children.

Delo owns an embroidery business called Delo and Stitch, and a food sourcing company called Ingredient Wizards, and also manages an import company. She also has led seminars and spoke in front of large groups for Landmark Worldwide, a company that redefines the very nature of what's possible.

After being diagnosed with breast cancer in September of 2016, Delo has made it her mission and passion to educate others on breast implant illness and also get involved with breast cancer organizations. Spreading awareness of the disease and also helping survivors and their families find relief in free services. Delo enjoys competing with her all-breast cancer survivor dragon boat team and CrossFit to stay in shape.

Connect with Delo:
Website: www.deloandstitch.com
Website: www.theingredientwizards.com
Website: www.neemtreeorganics.com

WAVE AFTER WAVE OF PINK

I Don't Do Wait and See Very Well

Kerry Farnham

I never thought I'd have to sit in a room like this again. Just 7 years ago, my husband and I sat in a similar small hospital conference room when we were told our 11-year-old son's chemo treatment failed and he would not survive without a bone marrow transplant. The same, surreal, out-of-body feeling I had then came rushing back. Over the next 2 years, I would apply many of the lessons learned with Sam's illness to my own; reading lab reports, reputable websites to use while searching for treatment options, working with insurance, dealing with neutropenia, accepting help, and journaling.

"The results of your biopsy confirm you have Invasive Ductal Carcinoma in both tumors found". I had convinced myself it would not be cancer. After all, I was only 48 and there was no history of breast cancer in my family. These words knocked the wind right out of me, and I knew my life would be forever changed, again.

I was given diagrams and a report I couldn't comprehend. There would be no tears shed, not yet. That would come later. For days and weeks after, I would lay in bed next to my husband, hoping he couldn't feel my body shake with silent sobs. But when he did, he just held me tight and let me cry. The lady continued to explain that although this type of cancer is very common, there was a complication. Both breast tumors were HER-2 positive and hormone receptor-positive. She explained that HER-2 meant aggressive, and in order to have the best possible outcome, treatment would also be aggressive. She gave the analogy of a 3-legged stool with each leg being a part of treatment: chemotherapy (full body and targeted), surgery, and radiation followed by hormone therapy. A whole year of my life would be spent on active cancer treatment. I had things to do, both professionally and personally. We had plans. We were going to attend my nephews' wedding in Las Vegas, and see Elton John, which I had been looking forward to for almost a year. Memories of my son enduring chemotherapy consumed my thoughts. I remembered how sick he got, the excruciating pain he endured, and how utterly helpless we felt watching him suffer.

When I was asked where I wanted treatment, I had no idea. I had been to our small, local cancer center for the first time about a month prior. I remember sitting next to a man who looked to be in his late 60s asking me what kind of cancer I had. "Oh, I don't have cancer. I'm just getting an iron infusion." It's ironic to think about that moment in time now. I needed time to process all of this, but there was a sense of urgency in her voice. I asked her to schedule with whoever could see me first, and if I didn't feel comfortable with the doctor, I would find someone else. Three days later on August 17th, I met with Dr. Forte. I immediately knew he was the right surgeon for me.

There were people who needed to know what was happening, starting with our children. We talked with our daughter, almost 12 at the time, and our 2 older sons. Next, I had my husband drive me to work. I was currently on leave after having an emergency hysterectomy 3 weeks prior, but school was starting the next day, and when you're an elementary teacher, there are a lot of details that need to be taken care of when you are going to be gone.

I remember walking into the building where I had been teaching since 1991. I had walked through the front doors of that old 2-story brick building thousands of times, but this felt different. I was suddenly filled with anxiety and was praying I would make it through the conversation I needed to have without breaking. The shock was starting to wear off and the realization of my new situation was setting in. So, with a deep breath, I walked in. The building was busy with all the day-before-school-starts preparations and excitement. I headed right for my principal's office and asked if we could talk in private. I took a deep breath, paused, and said those 4 life-changing words out loud. "I have breast cancer." This was the 3rd time I said those words, but the first time I cried. I am not one to cry in front of people, but there was no stopping the tears. I honestly don't remember much of our conversation, but I think he gave me a hug and told me not to worry about work. I asked him if he would read a letter from me at the staff meeting tomorrow. I told him my diagnosis was not going to be a secret, but I wanted everyone to hear it from me. I have been known to be a control freak, and with my life in a sudden tailspin, at least I had one thing I could control.

Over the next couple of days, I shared the news with my sister, brothers, and mom. Each time I thought I was ready to say the words, "I have cancer" without crying, and each time I failed. I sought support from my friend and neighbor, another breast cancer survivor, and my dear friend, Gayle, who had been battling breast cancer for decades. She was treated locally and knew all the doctors, so I leaned on her the most. Every time I had a question, she listened and gave me advice when I needed it. She kept me grounded, and every time I saw her at the cancer center, or the nurses brought me a gift Gayle had left, I felt a renewed strength. I love her dearly. I hope to use my experience to be a support for others the way she has always been there for me.

The next 2 weeks were filled with appointments and procedures including breast MRI, port placement, chemo school, and lymph node biopsy. Thankfully the lymph node biopsy came out clean. The chemotherapy I was going to have can cause heart issues, so I also had the first of many echocardiograms. I was thankful my days were busy. I was still healing from the hysterectomy, but I needed something on the calendar to do each day and focus on to keep from being swallowed up in my fear.

I felt very comfortable and safe with my medical team. I loved how my oncologist, Dr. Zhao, talked to us about the power of positive thinking and the important role attitude has in positive outcomes and healing. He also told us (my husband was with me and would be for almost every appointment and every chemo round) that he wanted me to start an aggressive chemotherapy treatment beginning September 7th. I would be given 4 different drugs: Taxotere, Carboplatin, Herceptin, and Perjeta. Treatment would be every 3 weeks for six rounds total. He gave me another stack of papers about each of these drugs. I spent several sleepless nights reading through everything and looking up terms I didn't understand. I was careful to stick to the medical sites I knew would give me the information I needed. Learning as much as I could was my way of trying to take control of an uncontrollable situation. Even though I was following the advice of my doctors, I knew I wanted to be in charge of my treatment and would not follow anyone blindly.

I was also very blessed to have a nurse who recently finished treatment for triple-positive breast cancer with a very similar treatment plan. I love all the nurses and staff who took care of me, but she really knew what I was feeling and fearing. She gave me insight, advice, and hope. Many tears were shed talking to Amanda, but I always felt strengthened and renewed afterward. Her survival and story helped carry me through some very dark times.

Dr. Zhao recommended having genetic testing done due to my age and lack of family history of breast cancer. This turned out to be a difficult process. Insurance refused to pay for the testing. But after 3 attempts and a change in the recommendation from the medical community, I finally got approval. This was very important to me, especially because I have a twin brother, a sister, and a daughter. I wanted them to have as much information as possible. It turns out I don't have any of the genetic markers tested, which was a relief, but still didn't answer the question of "Why did this happen?"

My insurance company again provided me with an amazing case manager. This was an invaluable service to us during my son's illness, and I was excited to have someone help me navigate the ins and outs of cancer treatment. Charlene was an oncology nurse and a Godsend. She helped me prepare for the TCHP chemo and its cumulative effects, gave terrific advice on how to help with the side effects, how to deal with insurance denials, and told me about different resources available. I took notes of every conversation, something else I had learned. This was such a valuable lesson because I would soon learn what chemo brain is and how seriously it affects your memory. Even now, I find myself having no recollection of conversations I had just hours before, and have trouble organizing my thoughts or finding the correct words to use when speaking. This has been one of the hardest things to cope with. I was able to deal with the horrible physical side effects because I knew it meant the chemo was working and they were only temporary. But the loss of my quick wit, ability to think on my feet, and remember conversations is something I still struggle with.

It was after my 2nd round of the TCHP that I lost my hair. I remember walking into the appointment for my second round, and Don, the CNA we all loved, commented as we walked down the hall, "How attached are you to your hair?" I knew I was going to lose it, but this was the first time we talked about it. "Well, I lost it before almost 10 years ago, so I guess it will be ok." When it started falling out, my husband contacted his friend, a hairstylist, and he cut my long, curly hair short. He did this two more times over the next couple of weeks until it was all gone. That final day I did shed a few silent tears, and my adoring husband stood by my side holding my hand. One more thing on hair. No matter how much you prepare for the loss, you still grieve. So much of our identity as women is focused on our hair, and when people see a bald woman, they see cancer. At first, I wasn't sure if I wanted to just wear hats and scarves, or get a wig. I decided to do all 3. For me, it was the right decision (I like variety and choices). Again, Charlene helped me get through this. A nice wig is expensive, and she worked very hard to get insurance to cover half the cost. I knew from my son's experience I would also lose my nose hair, which makes your nose run a lot, but I didn't think about my eyelashes and eyebrows. They go away too, and looking at myself in the mirror during that time was often unbearable.

By the third round of TCHP I wasn't sure I could go on. The bone pain, nausea, diarrhea, loss of taste, skin sores, neuropathy, and fatigue were physically and mentally debilitating. The side effects would really kick in about 3 days after each treatment and last for about 8 days. I would then feel functional for a few days until the next round. I tried to make the most out of the good days. It really does give you an appreciation for daily, mundane tasks like folding laundry, or the ability to go for a walk or meet up with a friend.

The TCHP chemo also left me neutropenic and I would often need transfusions between treatments. This took an emotional toll on us all. I am a positive person and try to always see the good in all situations. This was exhausting and frustrating. Treatment had to be postponed several times because my counts weren't high enough, and each time it was devastating. Grief and self-pity was a place I visited during these times, but I never lived there.

Cancer affects the whole family, and my heart broke for my husband. He wanted so much to take my pain away. I know how awful it is to watch someone you love suffer and not be able to do anything to help relieve their pain. Now he was going through it again. When I compare my experiences of going through cancer treatment myself and watching my son get sicker and weaker with each passing day, that helpless feeling of watching my son was more difficult. It was completely out of my control and I knew there was nothing I could do to alleviate his suffering. At least now I had a say and was an active participant in my treatment.

I was very blessed to have a strong support system, even when treatment dragged on an extra year. My work friends gave me a hat and scarf shower, and I received weekly cards and care packages in the mail. A meal train was started, and so many prayers were said for me and my family. My colleagues donated sick leave and we were given financial support when that leave ran out and I had to start paying my insurance out of pocket. Cancer is expensive! I put my pride aside when my sister wanted to start a Go-fund Me account to help with the cost of a specialty drug I would take later. As hard as it is to ask for and accept help, it is necessary. All the love we received from our family, friends, community, and strangers was overwhelming at times, and I will be forever grateful. It is a very humbling experience.

I have journaled off and on since I was a teenager, so this was not a new concept for me. But my journals in the past have always been private. Many years ago, a close friend of mine told me about the Caring Bridge website. I started posting updates during Sam's illness and found the entire process very therapeutic. Now, 7 years later, I would start writing on Caring Bridge again. Just like before, posting on Caring Bridge proved to be healing for me, both emotionally and spiritually. I gained strength from reading comments from people I loved and seeing how many "hearts" I had for each entry. It helped me feel connected to others and was a reminder I was never alone in my fight.

After the TCHP treatment was over, my husband and I met with Dr. Forte to go over the results of my latest breast MRI. The news was exactly what we had hoped for: I had a complete pathological response. We discussed surgery options and I chose a lumpectomy. On January 23, 2019, Dr. Forte removed the tissue around the tumor site along with 11 lymph nodes. Unfortunately, the margins weren't clear, and the following week I had to have surgery again to remove more breast tissue. All lymph nodes came back clear, but now I was at risk for lymphedema. I have friends who suffer from this and wanted to do everything I could to prevent it. Charlene came to the rescue again. She told me to seek out a physical therapist who specializes in lymphedema treatment. I didn't know that was even a thing, and I would have never thought of physical therapy. She also got insurance to cover the cost of a compression sleeve. Because of this preventative treatment, I do not have any swelling on my left arm.

As soon as I was healed up enough from the surgeries, I began 30 rounds of radiation followed by 11 rounds of targeted chemotherapy (Herceptin and Perjeta) every 3 weeks. It was a blessing to go through this part of the treatment! My medical team was right, I had endured the worst first. I was able to go back to teaching my 4th graders on April 29, and on September 20, 2019, I finished my last chemo infusion and I finally got to ring the bell.

Finishing active treatment is a strange feeling. On one hand, I was so relieved to be done and celebrated this accomplishment with my friends and family. On the other hand, it was like being adrift on a raft. I was just going where the current took me. I missed the comfort and security of going to the cancer center. I know that sounds strange, but during that time I was an active fighter. Now, I just have to wait and see, and I don't do wait and see very well. I needed to feel in control and actively fight any chance of reoccurrence. I did some more research and talked to my doctor about having an oophorectomy. Dr. Zhao, like always, supported my decision. My pathology showed a strong ER/PR component, so while this wouldn't get rid of all the hormones in my body, it would help. When I had my hysterectomy, I didn't know I had cancer so my ovaries were left intact. Now it was time for them to go. The surgery was successful, but I wasn't done yet. In my never-ending search for knowledge, I had become aware of a new drug used to lengthen the time before reoccurrence for HER 2 + cancers. Neratnib is an immunotherapy chemo pill that I would take for 1 year. When I brought this up to Dr. Zhao, he wasn't too sure as the side effects can be brutal, but if it was something I wanted, he would support my decision to try. So, while I was on leave recovering from the oophorectomy, I started Neratnib on November 2, 2019. Wow, brutal side effects was an understatement. I was bedridden for days and suffered from severe diarrhea and dehydration. My dosage was eventually reduced to a level I could tolerate, but I was still off work for 2 months. I was disappointed in my body for not being able to handle the full dosage because I wanted the full benefit. But I am glad to have had the opportunity to give myself every opportunity to prevent reoccurrence. To counter the side effects, I had to have weekly magnesium infusions from February 2020 – to November 2020. Thankfully, I could go in on Saturday mornings so I didn't have to miss work. Although I'm glad I have my Saturdays free again, I do miss the "me time" those infusions gave me, and I miss seeing the nursing staff I have become so fond of.

After chemo, I started on Arimidex. Because loss of bone density is a potential side effect, I had my first bone scan on Dec. 23, 2019. I went in to establish a baseline, so I was shocked when the tech informed me that I already had osteoporosis in several parts of my body. I was only 49. Dr. Zhao was equally surprised, and referred me to a specialist and switched me to Tamoxifen, which I have been able to tolerate well. It took almost 1 year to finally be seen, and I still don't have answers as to why this happened. Again, I have no family history. The specialist suggested Reclast, another infusion, to stop the progression. I agreed. I had my first infusion almost 1 year after that first bone scan and will have another one in a year. Just another reminder that my body will never be the same again.

Pink Sistas

A huge source of support during all of this was our church family. Several women in our congregation are breast cancer survivors, and one dear friend suggested I join the local support group. So in October 2018, 1 month after treatment started, I went to my first meeting. I didn't know anyone there and at that time I was the only one in active treatment. These women were exactly what I needed. They were survivors and took me under their wing. I looked forward to going each month and never missed a meeting, even when the side effects were hitting me hard. It was at one of these meetings I first met Deb Hart. She was our speaker for the evening and told us her story of loss and cancer. I felt a connection with her immediately. She spoke about her nonprofit, Pink Sistas, and the weekend retreats for cancer survivors she hosts on her beautiful floating home, for free! I knew I wanted to attend. Unfortunately, the retreat openings that summer were for a weekend I couldn't attend due to a work conference in California. It would be another year before I was finally able to attend her retreat. Because of COVID, the retreats were now just for the day, but what a glorious day it was. I met 3 other survivors and we ate, shared stories, did yoga, kayaked, paddle boarded (something I had always wanted to do), and went on a party boat ride. It was such a beautiful day with beautiful women and fed my soul. It was a time to just enjoy the day without any expectations, and I will forever be grateful for that experience.

Every day I think about my cancer. It's hard not to when I see the scars, pinprick tattoos from radiation, and feel the numbness at the incision sites. Cancer is a grieving process. I don't know if I will ever "get over it", but I have learned to live with it and not let it permeate every part of my life. Reoccurrence is still on my mind, but it will not stop me from living my best life. This is hard for a control freak like me, but I am getting better at it. Each day I put it further behind me, and now, my hope is to be a support for others who find themselves on this horrible cancer path. I want to use my experience and knowledge to give hope, support, and love to other women. I will never be the person I was before cancer, but I strive to be a better version due to the lessons I have learned with Sam's illness that I applied to my own. I have been on both sides: caregiver and patient. I will continue to use all my experiences to be more compassionate and empathetic to others, especially to those who look to me for guidance and support, and that is truly a gift.

Kerry Farnham

Kerry Farnham was born in Chicago. Her parents and twin brother moved to Montana before her 1st birthday.

Kerry and her twin brother, along with her younger brother and sister, grew up in a close-knit family where she learned the importance of service to the community and friends.

Kerry earned her bachelor's degree from Augustana College (now Augustana University) in Sioux Falls, SD, where she met her husband of 30 years, Troy. She also earned a Master's Degree from the University of Portland and is a nationally certified teacher. She and Troy have three children, one daughter-in-law, and 1 grandson.

Kerry enjoys traveling, reading, watching movies, and spending time with friends and family (especially at the beach). She also enjoys walking and hiking. She cherishes her annual vacation with friends from high school. Kerry is an active member of her church and plays in the handbell choir with her daughter, Anna, and son, Ian.

Kerry was diagnosed with triple-positive breast cancer at age 48 with no family history. She is an advocate for breast cancer research and the importance of annual screening through mammograms. Kerry strives to be a positive role model for others who receive a cancer diagnosis. She is strong in her faith and attributes her survival to her faith in God and never-ending support from her family (especially her husband, Troy), and lifelong friends.

Connect with Kerry:
Facebook: Kerry Martin-Farnham

WAVE AFTER WAVE OF PINK

A Year to Remember

Lauren Oman

Here we are. It's 2020, this is going to be the best year, a year to remember. Well, I got one of those statements correct.

* * *

January 23, 2020

Happy 40th birthday to me! Wow, forty . . . what should I do to celebrate this milestone? I know, I'll get my first ever mammogram. It's what you're supposed to do when you turn forty, right? In hindsight, I am so happy I decided to get one. I didn't know it at the time, but my whole year was about to change.

February 28, 2020

It's mammogram time. I had heard stories about mammograms being uncomfortable or even painful so I was a little hesitant, but the nursing staff was very polite and reassured me everything would be okay. They were very nice and described the whole process as it went along. It ended up being a piece of cake. No pain, no discomfort.

Once the mammogram was finished, I asked the technician if she saw anything on the scan, even though I knew she couldn't tell me anything. She said sometimes with dense breasts, which I had, extra imaging was sometimes needed. I didn't think much of it, just a mental note to be prepared—I might have to come back for some more images.

Three days later, I received a call and indeed, they asked me to come back for another mammogram because the radiologist had noticed some suspicious areas on my left breast. Most likely calcifications, but they wanted to make sure to rule everything out since I had thyroid cancer two years ago.

March 6, 2020

My second mammogram visit for the targeted areas of suspicion went just like the first appointment, very smoothly. As they suspected, it was calcifications. A lot of women have them, so again I didn't worry. Three days later, my results were in. The areas looked suspicious enough to warrant a biopsy because of the shape and size of the grouping of calcifications.

At this point, I started to get a little worried because the last time I had a biopsy it came back positive for cancer. But I wasn't going to let myself get worked up until I had the procedure done and had the results in hand. And, if it was cancer again, I would beat this one too.

March 19, 2020

Biopsy day. I had had biopsies before, so I thought I kind of knew what to expect. Boy, was I wrong? I lay on a cold hard table with my breasts hanging in a hole. Talk about letting ALL of your modesty go. The numbing process went smoothly, I hardly felt a thing, and luckily the same went for the actual biopsy. Just a little pressure and tugging. Three areas were biopsied and then the wait began. I should get my results within three to five days. Needless to say, I didn't get much sleep the days following the biopsy. A few days later, the results were back. NOT MALIGNANT, whoo-hoo! However, I wasn't out of the woods yet. The results came back as atypical epithelial hyperplasia, which is a precursor to cancer.

My surgeon wanted to go in again and take thicker margins with an excisional biopsy, to remove more tissue to ensure all the bad cells were gone. Okay, no problem, I need to do this.

During the same time, the dreaded COVID virus hit the US. Hospitals weren't performing any non-emergency procedures, so I had to wait to schedule my biopsy.

Fast forward almost three months. Hospitals are open again. Obviously, this whole time my diagnosis was on my mind. I was so relieved to finally be able to get an appointment and get this taken care of and over with.

June 4, 2020

Today is my excisional biopsy day. Out of the three suspicious areas, two of them were close enough together to be biopsied with one incision. My surgeon wasn't sure this would be the case until she got inside and saw the areas. Wires were placed, and a mammogram was taken so she knew exactly where to incise since the areas were microscopic. The surgery went well, the two areas were biopsied, and I was sent home to wait on the results.

My surgeon said if nothing was wrong, I would receive a call from her medical assistant, but if the results came back positive, she would call me herself. Jokingly she said, you DO NOT want me to call you. We had a good laugh since this was basically just a precaution—or so we thought.

June 8, 2020

It had been a long day at work, and I was done late. While driving home, I received a call from my surgeon's office. I answered it and when I heard my surgeon's voice, the tears immediately started to well up in my eyes. I remember saying, "Oooooh noooo," and her response was, "I'm so sorry I am the one calling you. "

The first question I asked her was if I was dying. She replied with a firm no, but this was something to be taken seriously. Two different types of cancer had been found, two of the areas were HER2+ cancer, and there was an area of Invasive Ductal Carcinoma (IDC) they didn't even know was there until the bigger margins were taken and processed.

Wow, I had cancer . . . again. We talked for what seemed a very long time; I don't even remember driving the rest of the way home. I knew I had to tell my boyfriend, family, and friends. They would be worried, and I didn't want that for them. I wasn't going to let this get the better of me. I had to fight as hard as I could.

I was referred to an oncologist I would meet in the upcoming week. So surreal . . . I have an oncologist. The day I met him I could tell immediately I was in great hands. I was going to be okay. He was very knowledgeable, very compassionate, and very detailed.

My oncologist suggested I get genetic testing done, since breast cancer runs in my family, and because of my prior cancer history. Luckily, after all the blood work and visits, my results came back negative for any abnormalities. He thought for sure my results would be positive, so this was a great surprise for both of us. Finally, a piece of good news.

I was given a few options for how we were going to go about treating my cancer. Chemo was definitely in my near future, as well as surgery. We just didn't know what type yet since they wanted to do a breast MRI of both sides to confirm the areas and see if anything new had appeared.

When I heard the word chemo, the first thing I asked is if I would lose my hair. That was really my main concern; after all, my hair was down to my lower back, and it was one of the things I was very proud of. He told me yes, I would lose all my hair, about two to three weeks after I started chemo. I started to cry, then apologized for being vain. He told me it was the number one question he was asked since sometimes our hair is what defines us as women and to never apologize. Hair grows back. I knew I had to get healthy and chemotherapy was hopefully going to be the answer.

June 19, 2020

Today was bilateral MRI day. Talk about claustrophobia. Facedown, again. On a hard table, again. With my breasts in a hole, again. Done. Okay, let's hope this turns out positive. I really wanted to get the treatment started right away.

A few days later, my results were in. The left breast confirmed the suspicious masses and a lymph node in my left armpit looked bigger than normal. The right breast also had a suspicious-looking mass they didn't see before. Oh, my goodness, what was happening?

Chemo was scheduled to begin in July, but they had to figure out what drug and dosage were going to be administered since they kept finding new abnormalities. Both of my surgeons thought an ultrasound-guided biopsy of all three areas would be best in determining the type of chemotherapy I would receive and the type of surgery I would have after my chemotherapy was complete.

Since I would be getting many infusions, my oncologist suggested I get a chemo port placed instead of having to inject the drugs in my arm every time. At this point, I was going to do whatever he suggested.

By this time, I had already had lengthy conversations with my employer about what was happening and the fact I would be having to take a long medical leave of absence since my immune system would be compromised and COVID-19 was in full effect. Typically, you can work through chemotherapy treatments, but not during a pandemic. The end of June would be my last day at my job of twelve years.

July 1, 2020

At my follow-up appointment, my oncologist and I discussed my biopsy results a little further and he thought I would benefit by joining a clinical trial for my HER2 + breast cancer. With the research being done, they would be able to help other patients with a similar diagnosis. I had to think about it for a few days, but ultimately decided it would be a good thing to do. The only scary part was being randomized into a treatment category. Although I wasn't put into the group who would be receiving the new chemo drug, I was put into the standard-of-care group and I was happy about that.

Originally my treatment was going to be six chemo infusions: once every three weeks, along with two immunotherapy drugs.

With the clinical trial, I was going to be receiving chemo once a week for twelve weeks, and every third week an infusion of Perjeta and Herceptin. The two immunotherapy drugs would help my own immune system fight the cancer. These infusions would be every three weeks for a year.

I was on board and ready to go. Let's get this started.

July 2, 2020
Today was my chemo port placement day. I'd had a handful of surgeries before, so this would be no big deal. The port was placed in my right upper chest and a catheter was threaded through a vein in my neck down into my vena cava above my heart. Today was the day it all became real for me. Now, I was officially ready to go.

July 3, 2020
For my bilateral ultrasound-guided biopsies, I had wires placed again, and another mammogram to make sure the correct areas were prepared. The biopsy sites were identified. Left breast, left armpit lymph node, and right breast new suspicious area. Luckily, I felt nothing, and all went well. By this time, I was a pro.

July 8, 2020
The results from the biopsies came back. The cancer had spread to my lymph nodes under my arm, but the mass in the right breast was benign. Having cancer in one breast is bad enough; thank goodness it wasn't both. More good news. I also got the news I was approved for the clinical trial and I would be starting chemotherapy the following week. I was so ready to be done with tests and to just begin my treatment.

Since I knew, I was going to lose my hair, I made an appointment that weekend to get it cut super short to donate to a charity. I cried, but then realized I didn't look so bad with short hair, it was kind of fun. Too bad it was going to all fallout.

Thus far during my journey, I had so many people reach out to me with positive thoughts, prayers, and advice. One of my friends told me about this wonderful lady named Deb who ran a nonprofit retreat for cancer survivors. Since I hadn't even started treatment yet, I didn't know what to expect when I contacted her, but to my surprise, she suggested we do a "chemo-sendo" party on her riverboat. I got to invite my friends and family and we spent a few hours on the river talking, laughing, eating, and just having fun before my upcoming journey. It really was a blessing and it meant so much to me. I am excited to do an actual retreat after I beat this cancer. Thank you, Deb, your kindness and strength are an inspiration.

July 15, 2020

Today was the first day of my 12-week chemo and immunotherapy journey. Boy, was I anxious, scared, and excited to get it started. Since they didn't know how I would react to any of the drugs being administered the day was very long and tiring. Nine hours, in fact. I had to get my loading doses and the nurses monitored me very closely to make sure I had no side effects, which I didn't. The infusions went very well, better than I was expecting. No problems to report. I was hoping this would be the case the whole time. The next day I woke up and I felt great, even went for a few miles walk with some girlfriends. WOW, I thought, this is great. Boy, was I in for a rude awakening? The next day I could barely get out of bed, I was so tired. My skin had also developed a weird bumpy rash, but thankfully it went away in two days and never reappeared throughout the rest of the twelve weeks. That loading dose was no joke. Or it could have been the steroids I got as a premedication before every infusion.

As the weeks went on, and the infusions became a part of my weekly routine, the fatigue really began to kick in, especially after the weeks where I would receive all three drugs. I would inevitably be in bed for two days afterward. I also received Benadryl as a premedication, which contributed to the sleepiness, but the chemotherapy was the major culprit.

By week three, sure enough, my hair started to slowly fall out. Every time I would run my fingers through it, I would come away with a handful of hair. I took a shower one day, and the amount of hair that fell out was astonishing. It literally happened overnight. I was in shock, but I knew it was going to happen, so I told myself to pull it together, and it will grow back. As the days went on, with every shower, more and more hair fell out . . . in handfuls. By the third day of "hair-mageddon," I asked my boyfriend to just shave the remaining hair off. I video messaged my mom and sister, and we had a good laugh-and-cry session as we said goodbye to my hair. Thankfully, to my surprise, my bald head didn't look too bad.

The only other side effects I had the whole time were some pretty harsh intestinal issues, brought on by the chemo and Perjeta (immunotherapy drug). Luckily, I was able to somewhat control it. It's still a bit of an issue but should go away once I stop all of my infusions. I cannot wait for that day. I feel like I was pretty lucky. I never got sick, I didn't feel sick, despite the fact I had aggressive Stage II cancer. With all I was going through, my oncologist kept telling me how lucky I was since it was a fluke that I even had a mammogram in the first place. I agree with him.

Towards the end of my chemotherapy treatments, I had several appointments with my general surgeon and plastic surgeon to discuss my surgery options. One of the options was to have a double mastectomy with reconstruction, and the other was to have a lumpectomy and bilateral reduction and lift. From the beginning of this ordeal, breast conservation was the opinion and goal of both surgeons. The risks, pros, and cons were given to me for both options and now I had a decision to make. My first thought was to go for the double mastectomy. Just get both breasts removed, have reconstruction, end of story. My surgeon and oncologist told me to think hard about it because reconstruction wasn't always what people thought it would be. I also found out that I would have to have radiation after my surgery since the cancer had spread to my lymph nodes. Decisions, decisions.

September 29, 2020

MY LAST CHEMO INFUSION. I can't believe how quickly those twelve weeks went. Now I had a break for a month to get my immune system back to normal before my surgery. I also had to make a surgical decision. Time was moving fast.

October 9, 2020

I had a follow-up MRI today to see if the chemo had done its job. Sure enough, all the masses and the lymph nodes had shrunk and were back to normal size. There were no other signs of abnormalities. The chemo worked. Thank goodness. Since everything had shrunk, the best surgical option for me would be to save my breasts, but because of the size of the areas where the cancer was, I was told my plastic surgeon would have to be creative at the time of removal and reconstruction. I was ready.

October 14, 2020

I met my radiation oncologist today. Since radiation was necessary with either surgical path, I knew I had made the right decision. She was pretty positive that radiation would be the best thing for me for preventing a recurrence of cancer. Radiation would consist of five weeks of treatments, Monday through Friday. The treatments would start after my surgery.

October 28, 2020

Surgery day. For most of my adult life, I had always wanted to get a breast reduction, this just wasn't how I wanted to have it happen, but there is always a silver lining when it's free! My surgery, a partial mastectomy of the left breast, bilateral reduction and lift, and the removal of six lymph nodes in my left armpit, was about five hours long. Because of COVID, I wasn't allowed to have anyone in the room with me, so I woke up alone.

I was told the surgery went very well, and I had wonderful new boobs. I stayed one night in the hospital, with no pain throughout the night or the next morning. My plastic surgeon came by the next day to check on me and I got to see my new breasts for the first time. I was very pleased; he had done an exceptional job. They were perfect. The only downfall was I had two drains, one in each breast. I had to take care of the drains and empty them three times a day for the next week. It wasn't as bad as I thought. I had very little pain. I wasn't allowed to lift my arms or lift anything heavy for a week. I healed very well. After a week I had the stitches and drains removed, and my surgeon said I was healing ahead of schedule. I'll take it.

Once again, my body had to heal. After about three weeks, I was almost back to normal, with no pain at all. Some soreness and twinges were all I experienced. I felt very lucky. What an experience this has been so far.

November 6, 2020

The surgery results were back, and I had no more cancer in my body. I could finally take a deep breath. There was a light at the end of this very dark tunnel I was in.

December 15, 2020

My first day of radiation. Because the area to be irradiated was close to my heart and lungs, I would have to do what is called the hold breath technique while the radiation was being administered. The hold breath technique entails your nose being plugged, and then breathing through a snorkel, until the time of radiation, then you take two breaths and one deep breath and hold it for about 20–30 seconds. This would be my life for the next five weeks. On the first day, I was very nervous because I didn't know if I could hold my breath for that long. Multiple times during each treatment. It was easier than I thought. It took them longer to set me up than the actual time the treatment took.

So far, I have a little swelling, some redness, and some fatigue, but no significant side effects. I will take this as a blessing in disguise.

I have been very fortunate in all of my treatment and I am so thankful I made the decision to go and get a mammogram. It was probably my best decision yet. I have so much life ahead of me and I can't wait to be done and healthy again.

Much love and peace!

Lauren Oman

Lauren Oman has worked as a dental assistant for the past 20 years, a job she loves. Lauren and her boyfriend Matt enjoy the outdoors; fishing, clamming, crabbing, hunting, going to the beach, and spending time on their boat. She also loves dogs and enjoys quilting, crafting, and painting.

It was June 2020 when they diagnosed Lauren with Stage II HER2 Positive cancer, and Invasive Ductal Carcinoma. The cancer had also spread to the lymph nodes in her left arm.

Lauren went through twelve consecutive weeks of chemotherapy. She had a partial mastectomy of the left breast with bi-lateral reconstruction, and twenty-five rounds of radiation. She also had a year of immunotherapy infusions that were completed in July 2021.

Lauren had no symptoms at her very first mammogram when she received the breast cancer diagnosis. Because of this, she advocates and encourages women to have mammograms.

In July 2021, Lauren completed her last immunotherapy infusion, which consisted of every three weeks for a year.

Lauren had her 6-month post-radiation mammogram in September 2021. The results showed no sign of reoccurrence and very healthy tissue.

Support from loving family and friends helped Lauren get through this very scary time in her life.

Connect with Lauren:
Email: Honeygirl10@hotmail.com
Instagram: @frogger12345
Website: https://laurenoman.po.sh

WAVE AFTER WAVE OF PINK

The Storm

Deb Hart

Seven months after I lost my twenty-two-year-old son, Kasey, I was diagnosed with breast cancer. I had only been married for a few months before Kasey died. This new relationship was based on the fun-loving, life-of-the-party girl who was foot-loose and fancy-free, financially independent, and ready to live life now that the kids were gone. I was young, healthy, and happy. I was these things, and in the span of just a few months, I didn't know who or what I was.

Wow! Breasts removed. Chemotherapy. Infections. Had just lost my son. To say I was not a good parent would be an understatement of gross proportions. ***I barely had any will to get up each morning, let alone to rebuild, relive, or reconstruct.*** However, time marches on. At the beginning of this story, I struggled just to get out of bed and take a shower. In the end, I wrote a book, started a non-profit, and became an inspirational speaker. In between, I got new boobies. Obviously, there's more to the story!

In the train-wreck stage of things, even my new rack was a disaster. My reconstruction was ok for about five years, and then my implants encapsulated, (which means scar tissue was forming and hardening around the implants). I had hunched shoulders and pain, not to mention they did not look good. So, I found a physician who claimed he could fix me right up! We had the damn things removed and replaced with the more natural lipo fat implants. Well, wouldn't you know it, this too went sideways. Because somehow, despite a "successful" surgery, two days after arriving home my kidneys failed. Subsequently, my heart failed, although by then I was in the ICU and they were able to revive me. Not so for the kidneys. I was sent home from the hospital after three weeks, to a life of dialysis three times a week for five hours a day. I was told there was a chance my kidneys would "kick back in." But for three months, this was my new so-called "life".

Like many before me, I was desperate to find a reason – some purpose for all that I was going through, so I bargained and made a deal with God. I promised if he would just get those kidneys going again, I would start a non-profit to provide retreats for women diagnosed with breast cancer I would write a book. I would become an inspirational speaker. The powers that be must have liked those ideas because the kidneys started working again. I wrote a book. I started a successful 501(c)3: *"Pink Sistas"*, and I am an inspirational speaker.

The second marriage failed (go figure)! But the new breasts are pretty good. I was nervous about them, especially being back out on the dating scene. But I did a little research and found a woman who did breast reconstruction nipple tattoos. For me, this was the key to just possible accepting, and maybe even liking my bosom! The tattoos make me think I have something resembling real breasts, and in the shadowy light of intimacy, they actually feel "real."

As for my life, I got it back by giving back.... I love the creativity and heart within the process of reaching out and supporting others. Every time I share my story, I come closer to healing my heart. Our friends and family want to be there and want to help us, but they haven't "done the journey." It is very different to be able to speak with someone who has suffered the same kind of challenge, the same kind of loss that you are experiencing.

During treatment and surgery, our families are there for us. After this, it seems that everyone offers the "high-five", sending cards, messages, or food. There is then a period where family and friends feel "we were there for you", but the process continues.

As we hop out of the shower and see that our breasts are gone.... these are the moments when the processing begins. We begin to the voice on our shoulder saying "when is it going to come back?" "How do I get my life back together?"

When you join with other breast cancer patients, there is a sisterhood that does not end amid your processing, but instead reaches a hand out to every stage of dealing with breast cancer and its aftermath. There is no judgment, only understanding. Do not put a timeline on your processes.

Joy and happiness will come back. Don't expect them to be there every moment. It's ok; this is a true hit to self-confidence and self-image. Allow yourself to be nurtured and cared for as much as your life allows for this.

Deb Hart is the founder of **Pink Sistas, Inc.**

Deb is an inspirational speaker, mother, mentor, friend, breast cancer survivor, and breast cancer survivor confidant.

Pink Sistas is a 501(c)3 non-profit corporation dedicated to raising funds for no-cost retreats for women who have been diagnosed with breast cancer.

Pink Sistas retreats focus on healing after diagnosis of breast cancer through many activities: networking with others, yoga, art, kayaking and paddleboarding, social outings, and much-needed rest and relaxation.

Connect with Deb:
Facebook: Pink Sistas
Email: inspirationaldebhart@msn.com
Website: www.pinksistas.org

WAVE AFTER WAVE OF PINK

The Choice Does Not Belong to Fate

Amber Christine Conner

"You either get bitter or you get better. It's that simple. You either take what has been dealt to you and allow it to make you a better person, or you allow it to tear you down. The choice does not belong to fate, it belongs to you." — *Josh Shipp*

I have heard different versions of the above quote throughout my life. I have tried to apply this idea to the challenges that have come along in my life. Each time I have learned something new, either about myself, about the world around me, or about other people in my life.

Without realizing it, I became a little bit stronger every time. All of the difficulties and hardships I've had to overcome led me to the moment when I got my breast cancer diagnosis. I never realized how much I learned about myself during the whole process.

I believe that if I am able to help even just one other person through their own hardship or challenge, then it was all worth the pain, suffering, ups and downs, and sickness that I faced. Even better yet, I wished that I was able to set a good example for my daughters, my daughter-in-law, and granddaughters. I hope that they never have to get a breast cancer diagnosis or that there will be even more advancements in the medical field on finding, treating, and even better; a cure for all the different types of breast cancer!

I tell you, some of those down days were tough, and I mean really bad! From being incredibly sick and lethargic and weak, I never could have won this battle with breast cancer on my own. I feel fortunate to of had so much love and support from so many wonderful people.

My husband Tony was with me through every single step of my battle with cancer. He was, has been, and still is my rock; I am thankful each and every day to have such an amazing partner. He has been in my life from the very first day we met, all those years ago in September of 1992. Our story is a miraculous love story of its very own! Every challenge along the way we faced together, these have helped strengthen our marriage.

I remember that day in June 2018 when I got the call with my biopsy results. Deep down inside, I already knew what the results would be, but I still had a little hope my intuition was wrong. But the dreaded phone call confirmed my suspicions, the small dimpling on my left breast was cancer.

When I got off the phone, at first, I felt numb and as if this moment was not really happening. But it was! I was home alone, and after a few minutes, I just broke down and cried. I had no idea what was going to happen next.

When you hear the word cancer, you almost automatically think, "I am going to die." I had to remind myself that cancer is not necessarily a death sentence. My husband was diagnosed with colon cancer a few years earlier; we made it through that fight, and he is currently 8 years cancer-free.

It is crazy how fast things went for me in the beginning. I have always been very diligent in doing my monthly self-breast exam. I had found a little dimple during one of my exams and I saw my primary physician a month after my discovery.

My doctor and I both hoped it was just cellular changes that can happen as a woman gets older and is reaching menopausal age. She, Doctor Claudine Moreno, was able to get me a mammogram appointment the very same day at Providence Cancer Institute Franz Breast Care Clinic. It felt like I was in a dream state as I walked from her office to the hospital where the Breast Care Clinic was located.

I was quickly escorted in for my mammogram. After the exam, I was directed to one of the changing rooms to wait for someone who would let me know if they found anything suspicious. I could tell by the technician's demeanor they had found something. I can read people pretty well without them having to say a word to me and I was right.

Out of kindness, they squeezed me in for an ultrasound so I would not have to come back for a second appointment. I had about an hour to wait before the ultrasound; I used that time to call my husband. He helped to calm me down and reminded me of our saying, "It is not a problem until it is actually a problem. Then we will deal with it one day at a time."

The ultrasound confirmed there was something suspicious in my breast and I had a biopsy right away. The doctor that performed the biopsy did his best to keep me calm and told me it could still be something other than cancer. He assured me that he would call as soon as he got the results. A few days later, he called me early in the morning with the official diagnosis of breast cancer.

My official diagnosis was Stage 1 Invasive Ductal Carcinoma (IDC). It was not very big, but it was right under the nipple and the surgeon had to remove all of my left breast, plus the lymph nodes. One of the lymph nodes tested positive for cancer cells, so I would have to undergo both chemo and radiation.

What? How can that be? I have no family history of breast cancer. In fact, no one in my family history has had any cancers. I went completely numb. One moment I was getting ready for work, and the next I got life-changing news. I feel so bad for the doctors who have to deliver this type of news to their patients. I had only met him one time, but I could tell he hated telling me bad news just as much as I hated receiving it.

I remember breaking down in my kitchen, crying, scared, and a little in shock as everything became real. My first call was to my husband; he had already left for work that day. Fortunately, he works close by; he left work immediately and came home because he knew I needed him. When he arrived, he scooped me up into his arms and gave me the best hug ever. He helped me calm down and reminded me we would take one thing and one day at a time. We applied this strategy when he faced his cancer battle, and we have continued to use it whenever something tough comes along.

By the end of the day, my surgeon's office, Kelvin Yu MD FACS, called with an appointment, and I set up another with my oncologist, Rui Li MD Ph.D. The next thing I knew, I was having my mastectomy, and my surgery just happened to land on our anniversary. Our anniversary was spent in a hospital room putting a few of those wedding vows in play. For better or worse and sickness and health! I had a single mastectomy on my left side. I also had an expander placed during my mastectomy surgery because I planned on reconstruction surgery later on.

I was afraid of how my husband Tony would react to losing my breast and all the scarring, but he is the most supportive, loving, compassionate man I have ever met. He says that my scars make me even more beautiful because they tell my story and are there to remind me how strong I really am. I feel so incredibly blessed to have his love and support. He has become a great caregiver and, believe me, that has been tested almost every day since. I am still having a lot of complications from surgeries and treatments. He had been by my side every step of the way.

I am so thankful I also have my three amazing children. My son Taylor and my daughters Kayla and Alexis. They have been helpful, supportive, and cheered me on throughout my battle. My mom, Gayle, even made the journey from Eastern Oregon to stay in Portland to offer support.

I work as an Early Childhood Educator and the families of the children I work for were so kind to me during my surgery recovery. They even prepared a meal train for my family. I even had my aunt Carla bring us some amazing meals! So many people I barely knew or were perfect strangers helped us out. I was a little uncomfortable accepting help at first. I definitely learned a great lesson in humbly accepting help from others. I realized that there are a lot of wonderful people who wanted to show their love and support in any way they could. Even with all these incredible people in my life, I still felt kind of alone at times.

My husband Tony went through his own cancer battle; he could relate a little to me and what I was going through. He treated his cancer like it wasn't even there. He kept on telling me how he got through his battle and that I should do the same.

Everyone kept telling me how brave I was. I wasn't brave; I did not choose this. Bravery is when someone chooses to put themselves in harm's way in order to help others. Police officers, firefighters, those who join the military; people like that are brave!

I thought I had to put on a smiling face all the time. I could not allow any negative feelings or thoughts to get to me. I tried my hardest to stay positive all the time, even after I started chemotherapy in August.

Chemotherapy is tough, very tough! I went through eight rounds, each round piggybacking on the last. Every round would build up in my system, making the next round harder for my body and mind to get through. I always say I would not wish chemo on my worst enemy.

During the last four rounds of chemo, I was told there was a small chance of an allergic response to the chemotherapy medications. I wondered "How would I know?" Well, my body knew! Going into anaphylaxis was one of the scariest moments in my life. Almost instantly my throat started to close up and I had a hard time breathing. Afterward, I was teased a little about how I was just wanting some attention from all the nurses at once. Never had so many medical staff come running to my aid.

I finally had reconstruction surgery in February 2020. The expander was replaced by an implant. I knew that it was risky since I did not do so well with radiation. I burned so bad and there was a lot of damage and scarring. But I healed very well, and in August I finally went out and bought some nice bras and lingerie.

In September, I developed a wound on my reconstructed breast that would not heal. Between my plastic surgeon, primary physician, and express care doctor, I had four rounds of antibiotics. The wound looked better in early November, but it quickly went from bad to life-threatening. I saw my plastic surgeon on December 7th, and she admitted me to Providence hospital the same day. I was prescribed three days of I.V. antibiotics, then I chose to have surgery to remove the implant. My surgeon told me that I could have a new implant placed, but I did not want to go through the process again.

After five days in the hospital, I still needed another round of antibiotics. Now in the clear, I finally feel like myself again. I think my body was telling me something was wrong with my implant almost immediately. So many weird things going on with my health for months, but once the implant was removed, all the weird health issues were gone, too. My plastic surgeon was able to remove a lot of the damage inside of me, that caused me so much pain in me for almost two years.

Once again, I had to mourn the loss of my breast. Luckily, I have a wonderful husband, who loves me for me and not my outside. He has been supportive. He didn't want the reconstruction because he feared it would cause another painful dangerous surgery, but he knew I had to at least try. When I had to make the decision to try a new implant, he told me to shut my eyes and take three deep breaths and visualize how I would feel looking in the mirror tomorrow, six months from now, and then ten years from now. That really helped me. I realized that I am and will be happy without a breast-and I am! And my husband keeps my spirits up by saying that he loves the other breast twice as much. Which makes me smile inside and out.

I didn't comprehend how much the infection affected me, physically and mentally. The prescribed drugs had some bad side effects, but now I am off all the medications, and I feel like Amber again. "I am glad to finally have my wife back, "says Tony.

Now let me tell you how Pink Sistas came into my life. Just like everything else, my introduction to Pink Sistas, Deb Hart, and everything they do came quickly and out of the blue. With my permission, my mother gave my number to a recently diagnosed co-worker. I received a phone call from Bradley, now a member of the board, who does a lot of volunteer work for Pink Sistas. Briefly, she told me about Pink Sistas and the amazing retreat Deb had just hosted. I could tell by her voice and description that her experience was life-changing. Immediately after, I was on the phone with Deb Hart. You can hear and feel her radiant energy! She informed me about the who, what, when, where, and how's of Pink Sistas. She had one opening for the retreat the following weekend, and I signed up to go right then.

A few hours later, I expressed some doubts to my husband about attending the retreat. I had just completed my second round of chemo and lost all my hair. My third round would be just a few short days before going to the houseboat on the Columbia. I wouldn't know anyone. I would be feeling ill due to my recent treatment. My husband convinced me to go, so I did, though I would be out of my comfort zone.

On the day of the retreat, my husband dropped me off at the houseboat marina. He gave me a huge hug and a kiss and said to have fun, relax, and enjoy the little break I was getting from my usual routine. I grabbed my bag and headed down the walkway, following the signs leading to Deb's houseboat at the very end of the dock.

I walked in and followed the voices up the stairs to the main living area and kitchen. Right away I received a warm welcome from Deb and the other guests. My nervousness was short-lived. That weekend was so wonderful.

First; I got to meet some amazing women, each with their own personal experience with breast cancer and in various stages of their own battle. Some, like me, were in treatment; others were out. It was great to hear everyone's story and experience. I was able to use so much of what I learned from them in my own battle.

Second; Deb was an amazing host and took great care of me and all the guests. The food was delicious. The weekend was filled with fun activities. Painting wine glasses and making jewelry. A fun boat ride along the Columbia River. Paddleboarding and kayaking. Yoga outside on the dock was amazing! I learned so much more about what Pink Sistas is all about, firsthand.

When the weekend was over, I felt refreshed and relaxed, which gave me more strength to endure the rest of my treatments and win this round. I connected with some amazing women and made new life-long friends.

I continue to be involved with Pink Sistas. The organization is run entirely by dedicated volunteers who do this out of the goodness of their hearts, especially Deb Hart!

There are several events planned throughout the year. The biggest is their annual fundraising auction (both live and silent), an amazing event with food and live music.

The money from the auction and other fundraisers provides retreats to women diagnosed with breast cancer, at absolutely no cost to them. Pretty amazing, to be able to attend one of the retreats without having to worry about the cost!

Pink Sistas means so much to me and to so many others, I've received so much from them: sisterhood, advice, encouragement, strength, and most important of all, love!

Amber Conner

Amber Christine Conner was born and raised in the Great Pacific Northwest, where she developed a love of nature and the outdoors. Oregon, Washington, and the surrounding areas have a wonderfully diverse environment that provided many opportunities for camping, hiking, rafting, sledding, and so much more. Her favorite place of all is the Oregon Coast. She continues living in the same area today, exploring both old and new areas. She especially enjoys, when she and her husband can, going on mini weekend adventures within a few hours distance.

Amber met her husband, Tony Conner when she was sixteen years old. Since that very day that they met, they have been inseparable for almost thirty years now. In fact, they have spent less than a month apart in total over all these years. If there is a thing as love at first sight, then it was for them. Over the years that love has grown and become something so deep and rare. They are definitely soulmates!

She has raised three children with Tony, their son Taylor; and daughters Kayla and Alexis. They have each grown into incredible adults. Amber also had two grandsons and a granddaughter. Her children and grandchildren are her world. She loves her family unconditionally and gives her whole heart to them.

She worked as a Certified Medical Assistant in her early years. After the birth of her youngest, she felt blessed to be able to be a stay-at-home mom. During this time, she earned a degree in Early Childhood Education. It has become her passion in watching and helping young minds develop and grow. She has been lucky to have been able to watch many children grow from infants all the way to adulthood. She says that it is amazing to see them get married and have children of their own and feels that she had a little part in those early years, that helped them to become these wonderful adults.

Connect with Amber:
Email: mrsamberconner@gmail.com

WAVE AFTER WAVE OF PINK

What's your superpower?

Shannon Preston

In 2012, I had my first child, and I weighed almost 300 pounds. I had been obese for most of my life. Diets? I'd tried them all and failed. Or, at least if I'd managed to lose any significant amount of weight on them, I'd gain it all back, and then some once I quit.

A few weeks after my son was born, a friend, who'd had great success recently in losing weight asked me to join Weight Watchers with her. I begrudgingly agreed and spent the first six months just treading water, not making much progress.

One day, I resolved that I was going to finally stick with it. I honestly don't know what clicked, but it did. It took me three years, but I managed to lose over 140 pounds. I had taken up running, completed several 5k's, 8k's, and 10k's, and in 2015, I was invited to be on a Hood to Coast team for the first time in my life. If you've never heard of Hood to Coast (or HTC), it's a 199-mile relay run from the top of Mt. Hood to Seaside, OR. It spans about 35 hours, with teams of twelve and each team member runs three legs totaling around fifteen miles per person. It's such a magical and empowering experience, after my first relay, I was hooked.

The Hood to Coast is a highly coveted event, teams come from all over the world to compete - and the team selection is done by lottery, so it's not a guarantee that your team will get in. In 2018, I decided that I wanted to create a fundraising team, which guaranteed our entry, as long as we raised at least ten thousand dollars. The beneficiary of the Hood to Coast is Providence Cancer Institute. Our team ended up surpassing our goal and raised almost twenty thousand dollars in the first year. We signed up to fundraise again for the 2019 relay almost as soon as we finished that first year. We were on a roll and wanted to keep going.

I first found my lump in June of 2018. I was in the shower one day and noticed it by accident. Because of my major weight loss, I had a lot of very thin and sagging skin, and my hand ran over something that felt odd. I was breastfeeding my second child, at that time, and assumed it was a clogged milk duct. When it didn't go away, I made an appointment to see my primary care physician. She agreed that it felt like a clogged duct but sent me in for an ultrasound to have it looked at anyway. The ultrasound results were consistent with the cystic matter, and the radiologist suggested I come back for a follow-up ultrasound in six months.

In the meantime, I ran my first half marathon and then had a breast lift and tummy tuck, to remove all of that extra skin from my weight loss. I returned to running again within just a few weeks, and I was feeling great.

I probably would have forgotten to follow up with that ultrasound, but right on time, I received an email reminding me to schedule my appointment. I wasn't sure if I needed to schedule through the hospital directly, or through my physician's office, so it took a while to get the appointment. There was something nagging in my mind that made me work hard to make sure I went in for that follow-up. I had mentioned to a friend that sometimes when I was running, my upper left breast was sore. After days of trying, finally on my 36th birthday, I got through and booked the appointment. Honestly, the day I went in for that follow-up, I thought it would be routine, and I'd be in and out of there in a few minutes.

My world was turned upside down that day, Tuesday, February 19, 2019. At first, it felt like a routine exam, I've had my fair share of ultrasounds. It's normal to hear the buttons click as they are taking pictures of what they are looking at. Eventually, the technician asked me to take my arm out of the sleeve on my gown, so he could look in my armpit, and then the clicks started. I was silently thinking "what is in my armpit that he is looking at?" Once he was done, he said he was going to go get the radiologist to have her look at the pictures. He also asked if I had any history of breast cancer in my family, which caught me off guard. Before I knew it, I was having my very first mammogram, and then back to the ultrasound room to have a more in-depth look at my right breast. There were three places of interest to the radiologist and she had me scheduled for a biopsy the next morning. I'm not sure how I held it together as I walked out of the hospital, but as soon as I got in the car, I called my mom and burst into tears. "I can't have cancer; I have two little kids!!" was all I kept saying. She insisted that she would be attending the biopsy with me. After the doctor performed the biopsy the next day, she told me what she thought - that it was cancer. She listed a few different types that it looked like and said it would be confirmed with the pathology report which could take 5-7 days. Once she left the room, the tears started again, and I cried "I can't have cancer, I fundraise for cancer research! This isn't fair!"

I spent the next day in one of my favorite places, skiing with my stepmom, who had her own battle with breast cancer in 2002. She went through the gamut of chemo and had a mastectomy. She shared with me all of the things she had gone through. Today, I feel bad that I wasn't more involved when she was in treatment, I was just nineteen, and I didn't understand the magnitude of the situation. That entire day, I had a feeling that the results would come back as cancer. As soon as we got home that afternoon, I received a call confirming that I had Invasive Ductal Carcinoma, a common form of breast cancer. The rest of the day is a blur, but I clearly remember when my general physician called me, all she had to do was say my name, and I broke down. She's been my doctor since I was twelve years old, and it was like talking to my mom. She assured me that we would be fighting this. She gave me the names of some great oncology doctors that she wanted me to see right away.

The next two weeks were incredibly busy. At my first appointment with my medical oncologist, he told me I would have to have six rounds of TCHP chemotherapy, administered every three weeks, and then I would have either a lumpectomy or a mastectomy (my choice) after that. The first thing I did, was go through my calendar to make sure I'd be done in time to run Hood to Coast, and I told him that. He laughed at me. He probably thought I was insane! Here he was telling me I had stage 2, triple-positive breast cancer, and I was telling him about how my event at the end of August was going to need to be worked in. During those two weeks, I had a port catheter placed, so that chemotherapy could be administered, a PET scan to see if the cancer had spread to anywhere else in my body, a Breast MRI, an echocardiogram to get a baseline on my heart since chemo can cause heart failure.

On the day of my first chemo which was just 13 days after that follow-up ultrasound, I got up early and ran five miles before I took my son to school and headed to the doctor.

I was so lucky that my dad and stepmom insisted on taking my kids for the weekends when I was going through chemo. Having them at home would have been rough, I had my infusions on Wednesday, and by Friday, I was out of it, sleeping 20 hours of the day. Saturday and Sunday were miserable because I couldn't sleep or focus on reading or watching movies, the minutes took forever to pass. By Monday morning, I would force myself to get up and walk my son to school again. I usually would give myself about a week to recover before I would start running again, and I averaged about 30 miles in between each treatment. One week after my last treatment, I hosted our annual fundraising garage sale at my house. It was a lot of work, and I was exhausted, but it was for a great cause!

I also continued to get up and run on the morning of every infusion. My nurses started asking "how many miles did you run this morning" when I would get there.

As scheduled, I had my lumpectomy with axillary lymph node dissection on July 18th. The hope was that the chemo would have destroyed all of the cancer, but it wasn't completely wiped out. I still had a little bit remaining in my breast, and one of the nineteen lymph nodes that were removed was positive. Not all bad though, the surgeon was able to get all of it out and produce clear margins. Here's where it gets cool; there is a new treatment that was released in May of 2019 for patients that have HER2+, lower stage breast cancer, with residual cancer after chemo. It's called Kadcyla, and it's a mixture of a hormone suppression agent and mild chemotherapy, and it targets the HER2 cells and reduces the re-occurrence rate significantly. Previously it was only used in Stage 4 breast and lung cancer patients to prevent spread and prolong life. Remember that fundraising for cancer research I mentioned earlier? That's me, I am a direct beneficiary of cancer research! So, while I had to have 14 rounds of this Kadcyla stuff, which is an infusion that I received every three weeks, I'm so excited to know that my chances of having my cancer come back are so much lower.

Around the time of my surgery, I was contacted by Deb Hart. She had met with my uncle Brad looking for a boat motor donation for her pontoon boat. After she was finished telling him all about what Pink Sistas does, he told her that his niece was battling breast cancer currently and asked if she would be able to squeeze me in on a retreat weekend. She barely left his shop and was on the phone telling me all about her retreats. Not only did she find a space for me, but she found room for my friend Angela, who I had met through this cancer process. The retreat was the weekend before Hood to Coast and was also at a big decision point in my journey. I literally had just come from a radiation consultation. Through the entire process, I had always thought I would be able to skip radiation by having a mastectomy instead, but due to residual cancer at surgery, it was highly recommended I do 30 rounds of radiation. I'd also been given some conflicting information, so I was extremely confused. I had a wonderful time at Deb's gorgeous floating home. She takes hospitality to a whole new level by giving up all of her personal space to ten women every weekend. She is up at 5 AM starting the day with coffee, entertains the entire time, and never lets a guest lift a finger. I was able to make some friendships with a variety of other survivors, along with trying yoga on the dock for the first time. We took sunset cruises on the pontoon boat, laughed and cried together, made jewelry to keep as a reminder of our weekend together, and all for free. My wish is that every survivor can attend one of her retreats in their lifetime!

After my retreat weekend, I ran my fourth Hood to Coast! Our team finished our second fundraising year with over $18,000! During my daytime runs, I wore shirts that said "I'm kicking cancer's butt! What's your superpower?" and "Cancer picked the wrong Bitch!" on the back. I had numerous people give me words of encouragement as they passed me on each of my legs, and it meant so much. It's funny, the first year as a fundraising team, we thought we were raising money for a great cause. This year had a whole new meaning. Not only had I been diagnosed with breast cancer, but a 34-year-old teammate was diagnosed with testicular cancer in January, and his father had just been diagnosed with prostate cancer. I was the leg 12 runner, which meant I was the last runner on our team and got to finish along the boardwalk in Seaside with crowds cheering me on, and then ran onto the sand to meet the rest of my team to cross the finish line together. Finishing that run meant more to me than any prior year, I was determined to meet a goal, and I had achieved it.

I did end up going through 30 rounds of radiation and decided not to have the mastectomy. The reoccurrence rate if I'd had the surgery was only 1% better than it is with the other things we're doing. The radiation for me really wasn't terrible. I still have some pain in my left breast when I run, and I'm going to physical therapy for some after-effects in my arm from the surgery. I'm told it will get better, but it could take time, possibly years. I completed my second half marathon (Girlfriends Run for A Cure in Vancouver, WA) during radiation, and then my third half marathon in Las Vegas shortly after radiation was over. In 2019, I logged more miles than any prior year (over 900) - even when I was in the best shape of my life! If I hadn't been diagnosed, I wouldn't have had a reason to push myself this year. If my doctor hadn't laughed and told me I wouldn't likely be running HTC, I wouldn't have tried so hard to show him I would.

In 2020 I was inspired by Paula Harkin, one of the owners of Portland Running Company and Runwithpaula events to start a run streak. A run streak consists of running 365 consecutive days of one mile or more. Most days I ran at least three miles. We took a three-day road trip down to Arizona. I woke up at 5 AM and ran circles in the Red Lion parking lot until I got to a mile before our long day of driving. The next day, I woke up early in Las Vegas and ran on the strip. I completed my run streak on Christmas Eve and had a radical hysterectomy on December 28th.

My battle isn't over, I still have a few more infusions left of a drug called Zometa which protects my bones, and will be on oral hormone suppression therapy for the next ten years. At times my joints ache and I've gained some menopausal weight, but I'm a fighter and I'll get back to where I was when I started this process.

I think it happened to me because I can bring awareness, and positivity to a devastating diagnosis. I saw my life flash before my eyes, and now I don't take any experiences for granted. I cherish more moments with my kids, husband, friends, and family. I look into the horizon and admire my surroundings. I take new opportunities to try new things. It's important for me to show strength and perseverance in everything I do.

WAVE AFTER WAVE OF PINK

Shannon Preston

Shannon Preston lives in Oregon City, Oregon with her husband, their son Lucas, daughter Avery and their one-hundred-pound Labrador, Dexter.

She worked in the escrow industry for many years before making the decision to stay at home with her children.

Currently, she keeps busy as the bookkeeper for her husband's small business, a consultant for a vacation rental agency in Arizona, and is also the captain of her Hood to Coast fundraising team.

Her hobbies included running, snow skiing, camping, watching football with her family, and traveling to her vacation home in Arizona. She also enjoys searching for a fantastic Bloody Mary with friends.

Connect with Shannon:
Facebook: @ShannonPreston

WAVE AFTER WAVE OF PINK

In The Shadow
Miranda Brennan

Cancer touched my life at the age of 10. I watched my mother go through the stages of an aggressive melanoma in 1980; she was 34. Diagnosed in January, she underwent surgeries, skin grafts, chemo, radiation, and without fail, it attacked her brain. She was terminal and there was no hope. We lived in Bend, Oregon; however, my mother spent many months away in Portland, beginning in January of 1980, leaving my two brothers and me with neighbors, friends, whoever would take us in. Once she was back in Bend, she was in the hospital. I would visit her in the hospital and some days she could not see me. On others, she could not hear me or was silent around me. I did not understand what was happening. It was a confusing, helpless time in my childhood. All of this and my mother was gone by April 17, 1980.

We were left living with my grandmother, who also was unwell and died only months later of pneumonia. My brothers and I became Wards of the State. I was frustrated and angry because life was not fair, my mother was gone, my grandmother was gone-but I was here. I was bounced from foster home to foster home throughout my teen years. The Children's Service System separated my brothers and me. I lost contact with my older brother but stayed in touch with my younger brother and the family that adopted him. Some foster homes were good, some not so good. There was a great home and family that wanted to keep me and call me their own. They loved and treated me like I was part of their family. However, I would manage to sabotage our relationship after only two years. That was MY timeline, as I had what was said to be Attachment Disorder. I would stay in one place for a maximum of two years before I would manage to push my way out of any relationship. After 16 different placements in foster care, I finally graduated!

(Something caseworkers thought I would never do.) They said I was too emotional, too angry. But I did it, angry or not!

I moved back to Bend after living in a small town in Eastern Oregon. I attended community college and worked in retail. Being alone and living on my own I found I was lacking a place to call home. I needed to be grounded and find a family of my own. I had grown closer to my younger brother's parents, as I had always stayed in touch with my brother. I was blessed to also become a part of their family at the age of 20. In 1989, I met a man who loved me for who I was, faults and all! He calmed and comforted me, - something no one in my life had ever been able to do. I was less angry with him in my life. I became softer, finally able to love another person and allow him to love me. He was my soulmate and gave me the love I had been searching for my whole life. He was and still is my hero. Two years after we met, we married. We bought a house and filled it with three beautiful children: a daughter and two sons! Life was like a fairytale to me. Life was GOOD!

In October of 2004, I turned 34. I had carried that date with me since my mother's death. I often wondered how she felt at the age of 34, knowing she was dying so young and leaving her children. Not that she had a choice; the cancer had taken that from her and so much more. I could never imagine having my children watch and endure what I had to as a child! Every year I grew older, I felt a little sad for my mother. There is so much she missed in life including not watching her children grow up. I would hope she would have been proud of the way I turned out.

At the age of 38, I found a lump in my right breast. I was sure it was nothing. Although doing breast checks had always prepared me to detect that hard pea-like lump, I ignored it. For a YEAR! I began to have night sweats - severe night sweats! I would change my pajamas three times a night, soaking wet. This was my first symptom that something wasn't right. My doctor said I could be going into what I call, "mental-pause." What?? I was too young for that! The next year the true and undeniable symptom happened. The skin in my right breast began to pucker, pulling my nipple down. At this point, I could not dismiss the lump, the pucker, the sweats, the inevitable. I knew in my heart I had cancer but did not want to tell my husband how I was feeling.

I called to make an appointment with my doctor, stating that I had found a lump in my breast. I saw my doctor's nurse practitioner that morning. She confirmed that I did have a lump in my right breast and immediately sent me for a mammogram. Being uninsured, things were getting very scary. The thoughts rolled through my mind, "How am I going to afford this?" "I can't get sick. I have a family to take care of! three kids: ages 17, 11, and 8." I could NOT do this to them. Thoughts of me as a child watching my mother being ill and knowing I could not do anything to save her came to mind, and I began to get angry. Once again.

When I arrived at the medical center for the ultrasound a social worker greeted me. She had papers for us to sign to apply for the Oregon Health Plan's Breast and Cervical Cancer Program. I wasn't aware there was such a program. What a godsend! With the doctor bills I had racked up already in just a few office visits, I was seeing dollar signs instead of focusing on my health. During the ultrasound, the technician took pictures. I could see the cancer: a very white spot with spider veins coming from it. I knew then it was cancer, and I wasn't surprised. When the technician left the room and brought in another tech to read the ultrasound again, I really knew. My husband asked if it looked like cancer and the technician told us that he could not tell us if it was or wasn't cancer, that a biopsy would determine that, but he said, "it doesn't look good."

I sat there, biting my lip refusing to cry, while my husband had tears running down his face. He looked at me and said, "We can do this! We can fight this!" Only then did a tear sneak out. He was right, and I knew I was not alone. After my ultrasound, we met with a surgeon. As I waited for him in the cold, dark room, draped in a well-worn gown, I looked around. There were breast cancer posters, his credentials as a breast cancer specialist, self-exam instructions, and posters from the Heaven Can Wait 5k fundraisers. A light knock sounded on the door and he came in. He was tall, rather handsome - and oh, how awkward I felt. It was all surreal. The surgeon did the biopsy and I was on my way, with my thoughts, my wonders, and worries.

The next few days seemed like a whirlwind, but I went about my daily routine of waking up at 6:00 a.m. to go walking. It helped to clear my head - only this time thousands of thoughts ran through my mind and nothing good. I went through the what-ifs, the how-too, and came up with horrible scenarios. My doctor called while I was walking. I stopped, looked at my phone, and contemplated not answering it, as if this was all a bad dream. I answered it.... she had sadness in her voice and I knew it was not going to be a good phone call. She told me it was as I had feared: breast cancer. Which would later have a name, Stage 2, HER 2 Positive, Metastatic Carcinoma. She explained she had made an appointment to see an oncologist, the "Cancer Doctor," and he would guide me through my cancer journey. After our conversation, I kept walking, no tears, just walking and thinking how I wasn't surprised. Hadn't I been in the shadow of cancer all my life? To me, it was a little late in showing up. I expected to be younger like my mother. After all, I had passed the age of 34. In some childlike way, I had figured I was in the clear.

As I continued my walk, I was getting angry. How was my family going to feel? Scared? Upset? Angry? How was I going to tell them? How could I break their hearts as mine once was? While continuing my walk, I happened upon a chalk drawing. There were flowers and scribbles that looked to be from younger children, but smack dab in the middle were the words "PANIC BUTTON PRESS HERE," with a big dot in the middle!! I was so angry, how appropriate for me to see this, today of all days. I jumped up and down on that dot, twirling in circles cursing under my breath, swinging my arms! I'm sure if anyone drove by, or looked out their window they must have thought I was crazy! I was crazy and angry... filled with emotions I couldn't even put my finger on. I sat right there on the curb and sobbed.

Miranda Brennan

Miranda Brennan is a daughter of many, sister of three brothers, wife, and mother of three. She grew up in Oregon as a foster child and ward of the state from the age of 10 until she was 18.

She is also one of the one in eight women to be diagnosed with breast cancer. Her diagnosis came in August of 2010. Bend, Oregon is where she calls home with her husband and beautiful children. They are her light and hope, and strength that kept her fighting this disease when she was at her weakest.

Miranda believes everything happens for a reason; because of her childhood, she grew up to be a very strong woman, which she feels prepared her to be a fighter.

Thank you, Deb Hart, and Pink Sistas, for your inspiration and words of encouragement by allowing me to be a part of this great book. If I have a hand in touching one life with my story, then this journey will not have been in vain.

Connect with Miranda:
Email: omandi3@gmail.com
Facebook: Miranda Brennan
Instagram: @omandi69

WAVE AFTER WAVE OF PINK

Clothed in Dignity

Robyn McManama

I sometimes cannot believe it happened to me. That I was the one on the receiving end of a phone call hearing "you have cancer". It felt like time stood still, just for a moment I was on the outside watching this happen to someone else. And then it hit me - that it was me, that I was the one with cancer.

I was only 35 at the time I was diagnosed. Too young for regular mammograms. I was in for my annual exam with my nurse-midwife when she felt a lump in each of my breasts. She thought they were cysts but sent me in for a mammogram anyway. Afterward, multiple doctors said her gut instinct had saved my life. The biopsy determined a couple of days later that I had Stage II Invasive Ductal Carcinoma in my right breast that was growing at an 80% proliferation rate (this is how quickly a cancer cell copies its DNA and divides into 2 cells. The higher the number, the more aggressive it is). The lump in my left breast was benign. I remember being on the phone with the doctor who had done my biopsy, thinking that I had no idea what to do now. Was I supposed to call someone or go somewhere? My mind was racing but felt completely blank at the same time. Thankfully, the doctor told me she would get things started and she referred me to two different breast surgeons. Within a couple of hours, both offices had reached out to schedule an appointment.

From that point on everything was a whirlwind. After I decided on a surgical oncologist, it was port surgery, chemo class, picking up meds, telling people, researching side effects. In the middle of all that, my husband Ryan and I had to figure out how to tell our two daughters that their mom had breast cancer and that life was going to change drastically. Our daughters were 7 and 10 at the time. We never wanted them to feel left out or not a part of what was happening so we were very honest with them about my illness and how chemo would make me sick. Our younger daughter didn't fully understand what it all meant but our older one did and she took it hard, but we stressed that we would get through this if we all supported each other.

Our friends and family did not miss a beat and we were immediately wrapped with prayer, messages, meals, childcare, and anything else we could think of. No one should have to walk a cancer diagnosis alone and we were so grateful for our community and how they carried us when it was too hard for us to move on our own.

Chemotherapy

About 2 weeks after my diagnosis, I had my first round of chemotherapy. The cancer was characterized as triple positive (ER/PR/HER2+) so I was given TCHP (Taxol, Carboplatin, Herceptin, and Perjeta). I was prescribed 6 rounds of chemo given every 3 weeks. All things considered, I handled the first and second rounds of chemo well. I was fatigued, nauseous and my mouth lost all its tastebuds, but I was not overly sick. I had heard horror stories of how sick other patients had become from chemo, so I was very thankful. One memory that will always be special for our family was the day I decided it was time to shave my hair. It had begun falling out in clumps exactly two weeks after my first treatment and I knew I needed to take control of it rather than feel pain and loss every time I saw my hands full of hair. My husband and daughters took turns cutting my hair short and then finally shaving it. We laughed and cried together and my girls and I spent time trying on the different head coverings I had bought. In the end, the act of shaving my head was difficult but also empowering. My bald head was a symbol of what I was going through, and I wore it proudly.

Then things got a little rough after my third round of chemo. I thought I was doing well - it was spring break and we took our daughters to a Broadway show and then had plans to head up to our family's vacation home at Mt. Hood. However, after the show, my heart just didn't feel right. It was beating too quickly and irregularly. I was advised to head to the closest ER, and I was admitted just minutes after arriving. They did a battery of tests but were unable to diagnose what was going on. However, because I was currently going through chemotherapy, they decided to keep me for observation. Over the next couple of days, I was put through every heart and stress test they could think of. The only conclusion was that I was having a bad reaction to the Neulasta shot (to keep my white blood cell count from dropping) I received after each chemo, and they put me on beta-blockers. This seemed to do the trick and I was able to complete my last 3 rounds of chemo without any incident.

Time for Surgery

One of the many things I've learned is that there are many types of breast cancer and along with that, many different treatment plans. My triple-positive cancer was one of the most aggressive, which means chemo first. The goal is to stop it from spreading while also trying to shrink the tumors before surgery. One of the benefits of this was the extra time it gave me to research and decide what kind of surgery I would have (lumpectomy vs. mastectomy). I had also learned at the beginning of this journey that I was positive for a genetic mutation called RAD50. This gives me a higher predisposition for both breast and ovarian cancer. Because of this, my doctors and I decided on a bilateral mastectomy for my surgery. I had my last round of chemotherapy at the end of May and I was given a few weeks to rest and recover before surgery which thankfully lined up with a family trip to Hawaii. What a wonderful time that was! We celebrated, rested, and tried our best to leave our cares of cancer back at home.

My mastectomy surgery and recovery went well. My husband was my rock – he tracked my pain medications, made sure I ate, helped me move around, and charted my drain output (now that's true love). At the time of my mastectomy, it was not known if I would need radiation, so my reconstruction was delayed and I was given expanders in the meantime. If you want to know what it feels like to have breast expanders, just imagine two rocks strapped to your chest. They are hard and uncomfortable but have an important job to do. Unfortunately, about 4 months after the mastectomy, one of my expanders became infected. I got extremely sick and ended up in the hospital for 3 days before they decided to remove the expander, clean out the area and replace it with a new one. Thankfully that worked and I had no other issues with the expanders.

The findings after the mastectomy were that the cancer had not spread to my lymph nodes so radiation was not needed. However, I did have residual cancer left (the goal is a 100% response rate) so I was prescribed to start a new kind of chemotherapy called Kadcyla. The typical regimen for Kadcyla is an infusion every 3 weeks for 14 rounds. After my third round of this, my eyes had an allergic reaction that caused me to begin to lose my eyesight. Thankfully this was caught quickly and I was taken off of Kadcyla. I was put back on the previously prescribed regimen of Herceptin and Perjeta (targeted therapy) for a year.

In between my mastectomy and delayed reconstruction, I had a total hysterectomy. This was done prophylactically due to the genetic mutation. It has been a struggle to go into surgical menopause overnight at the age of 36. The menopause symptoms started up almost immediately, but I have been working with a naturopath who has me on supplements to help combat the symptoms which have helped a lot.

After a ton of research, I opted for a DIEP (deep inferior epigastric perforators) Flap reconstruction. This is a microvascular surgery that uses lower abdominal tissue, skin, and fat as the donor tissue (instead of implants). It is a 10–12-hour surgery that requires a night in the ICU for careful monitoring and then several more nights on the surgical recovery floor. Reconstruction is a very personal decision and after a lot of careful thought and conversations, I decided this was what was best for me.

I was scheduled to have my DIEP Flap in March 2020, just a few weeks after the world started to shut down due to COVID-19. As hospitals began to cancel non-emergent surgeries, I learned that mine too had been canceled. I understood why but was devastated. This surgery was meant to mark the end of the biggest part of my cancer journey and I was anxious to have it completed. Also, I was desperate to have those expanders removed!

Since I was one of the first surgeries to be canceled, I was lucky to later be one of the first ones to be rescheduled. In August I had my long-awaited DIEP Flap reconstruction surgery. It took 12 hours in total and went off without a hitch. The first night in the ICU was rough as the nurse had to check the flaps every 30 minutes, not giving me many opportunities for sleep. Thankfully, this only lasted for the first 24 hours and then the frequency of checks decreased to every hour for another 24 hours and then eventually every couple of hours.

The hard part about this type of reconstruction is that it involves two major surgical sites. I was not able to use my arms to move around and I had lost all use of my abdominal muscles as well. The next day, I learned quickly that the daytime ICU nurse was no-nonsense and was determined to show me that I was still able to move on my own. She helped me out of bed for the first time since surgery and got me sitting in a chair. When it came time to transfer me out of the ICU into a patient recovery room and the patient transporter arrived with the wheelchair, the nurse would not allow me to sit in it, instead, she insisted that I walk! So, walk I did, all the way to my new room – across the entire hospital, from one end to the other. Not only did she show me that I was able to walk that far, but I became famous for it! Over the next three days, every nurse that came into my room said they had heard about how I walked all the way from the ICU.

My last surgery was 4 months after the first part of the reconstruction. DIEP Flap is a multi-step process, with at least 2 revisions. By this time, I was experiencing major surgery fatigue. It is hard to stop life for surgery and spend weeks healing only to start over. I asked my plastic surgeon if there was any way he could combine the 2 revisions which he agreed to do. It made for a longer surgery and a tougher recovery but I'm very thankful to say that after 2 years of surgeries and treatments, there are no more on the horizon!

For now, I will continue taking an aromatase inhibitor for the next 5-7 years and will receive an infusion of Zometa every 6 months. These medications work to keep my bones strong, both to resist a recurrence from happening and to prevent osteoporosis from settling in.

Exercising through Treatment

I have always been an athlete and exercise has long been a part of my daily routine. In the beginning, I committed to myself that if I couldn't do anything else, I would at least go for a walk every. single. day. And walk I did. There were some days when I could only make it to the mailbox and back, but as I regained my strength after each procedure, I saw my walks grow in length. When I was strong enough, I would work my way back to my normal exercise routines. I'm so thankful that for the most part, I recovered from my treatments and surgeries quickly. I attribute that to the fact that every day if I couldn't do anything else, I at least got up and out for a short walk.

On the day of my diagnosis, my younger brother committed to me that as soon as I was healthy, we would complete a Half Ironman together (something that had long been on my bucket list). I can now officially call myself an Ironman! I trained hard for over six months and completed the race with my family and friends cheering me on. I'm proud to have done something after cancer that I'd never done before – I proved that not only could cancer not defeat me but that I am stronger than ever!

Pink Sistas

I first learned about Pink Sistas from a couple of girlfriends who had attended a retreat with Deb Hart. I connected with Deb and expressed interest in attending a retreat as well. Sadly, that has yet to happen because all social activities were suspended due to COVID-19. However, Deb has followed my story on social media and has always been very supportive and encouraging. I'm thankful to have connected with her and I look forward to being able to attend a retreat in the future!

What Comes Next

I think that all cancer survivors know that cancer is never "over" in the true sense of the word. Yes, active treatment and surgeries have ended. Yes, I've been declared NED (thank you, Jesus!). But cancer will always be a nagging thought in the back of my mind. Does that new pain mean that the cancer has metastasized? It will always be my reality that I could face a recurrence. And I will always be dealing with the long-term effects of the treatments and surgeries.

However, I am grateful for every day that I get to wake up and be a wife and mom. I'm thankful that I get to continue to watch my girls grow older. I'm grateful for how cancer pulled us closer together as a family. I'm grateful for the women I've met along the way, each with their own unique story that has bonded us into a tribe of warriors.

"She is clothed in dignity and strength and can laugh without fear of the future." Proverbs 31:25

Robyn McManama

Robyn McManama is a native Californian but has called Oregon her home for the past 20 years. She earned her BA degree in Business from the University of Oregon and for 10 years owned and ran two resale clothing stores until she decided to be home full-time with her daughters while they were young.

Robyn, her husband Ryan, and daughters Lilly and Samantha have an active lifestyle of bike riding, hiking, traveling, and adventuring together. She also now works part-time at her daughters' school helping to tutor children and substitute where needed.

Exercise has always been a priority and passion for Robyn and when she was diagnosed with breast cancer, she set her sights on completing a Half Ironman once she was done with treatment. She enjoys exercising daily, volunteering, and living a life that doesn't revolve quite so much around her diagnosis.

Robyn loves Jesus, her family, and her friends. She is thankful and grateful to get to wake up each morning and live out her life as fully as possible, knowing that each day is a gift.

Connect with Robyn:
Facebook: Robyn McManama
Instagram: @70.3aftercancer
(to follow her journey to complete her first Half Ironman)
Email: rlmcmanama@gmail.com

WAVE AFTER WAVE OF PINK

From One Peak to Another

Tara Lynn McGuire

The beginning of 2020 was a year full of hopes, dreams, and excitement; it was as if everything I had been working so hard for was finally coming together. But, the spring of the same year turned our worlds upside down and we experienced desperate and seemingly insurmountable circumstances. Owners of a yoga center and a holistic health spa, my husband and I had just opened our second location – a large, state-of-the-art, hot yoga studio - and were well on track to reach, or exceed, our projections, including franchising, by the end of the year. Then Covid arrived and everything changed, as lockdown after lockdown and impossible-to-meet restrictions were imposed. I immediately went to work to create a virtual yoga platform and worked tirelessly for months to make it viable.

In August, in an attempt to hustle for rent, I created a women's fashion boutique in the new studio storefront. I was working harder than I ever had in my life, and I was mad at everything. I was mad at the staff and clients who treated me unkindly, at the utility companies for being rigid, at the government because their 'bailouts' were just loans and not much help at all. I was mad at our governing officials for their ridiculous management of the situations at hand. And, if I am honest, I was mad at God. I had never felt so much accumulated anger in my life.

It seemed as if nothing was going to get better soon, and in September 2020, I had to cancel my private health insurance and I applied for Medicaid. I no longer could justify putting $500 a month on my credit card with no hope of paying it off. There was a glitch in processing my application and in October, I still didn't have my number or a card.

One day in October, while drying off after a shower, I thought I saw a shadow on my right breast. I lifted my arm, examined the area carefully, and found no abnormality. In my early 40s, I had informed my gynecologist that I would not be doing routine mammograms, and I would like her to guide me to infrared imaging. She told me my breasts were soft and small enough that self-exam should be fine, as long as I did so regularly. She even showed me how to do a good exam. Fast forward to a shower in late November, and I thought I saw the same shadow in the mirror. Again, my self-examination revealed nothing. A week or so later, I was doing some yoga poses in my bedroom, wearing a loose pajama top. I saw my right breast upside down and my heart nearly stopped. I knew. My right breast looked dimpled, and the nipple pulled slightly to the right when I was upside down.

That night, as I assumed my normal shoulder lying and hugging position against my husband, a few tears streamed down, but I said nothing. Once I rolled onto my back, I began a vigorous exam. There were two lumps. My blood ran cold. I don't know how I got any sleep that night, or if I did. That night is a blur to me.

The next day, in our shared office, I angrily told my husband that I had to get a mammogram. He said, "Why would you do that?" I told him about the lumps. I could feel his energy shift as another unbearable situation was loaded onto his already burdened shoulders. He had been having rising PSA numbers for over a year, and we had been doing everything we could to sort that out in a healthy way. His father had cancer and died in my husband's arms when he was just 17 years old. He and I had made our lives about health and healing, and we had formed plenty of opinions about cancer treatments. When I told him about the lumps, my husband heard the catch in my voice and read my body language, and he could tell that was not the time to discuss it.

Next, I placed a panicked call to DHS to beg for help in getting my insurance set up. I cried on the phone as I explained I need a mammogram right away, and I needed them to clear up the insurance problem so I could get my ID. Thankfully, they helped push it through, and finally, on December 29th, I was able to get a voice call with a primary physician that I had never met.

During the call, I had zero ability to speak clearly to her and I apologized upfront, explaining I have a rare movement disorder that can strangle my voice on a good day - and this was not a good day. I managed to choke out my story, and I could feel her heartbreak for me. She referred me to an imaging center but, due to the pandemic, the first availability was weeks away. I was more than panicked at this point as over a month had already passed. I prayed, "God, please be with me and guide me to the right place for the right care. I am completely ignorant and completely overwhelmed, but I trust your guide and lead." I called other imaging centers and discovered the earliest availability would be at Oregon Health & Science University's Breast Clinic. I took comfort in that because I had worked with specialists at OHSU in an attempt to get to the bottom of my rare genetic disorders. While they never reached any definitive conclusion, they did treat me well. So, OHSU it would be. But I had another week to wait before the mammogram.

Somehow, just having the meltdown on the phone with the doctor helped me. I remember having that week to really process my thoughts. I felt anger at the breast cancer. I felt the most anger at COVID for giving me breast cancer. I knew all the anger I had been drowning in had fed this beast, and as a yoga teacher, and the daughter of a preacher, I was tempted to blame myself for allowing myself to become that angry. But I immediately knew better. I was doing the best I could, and it was a lot better than many people could have done. I would not take on any self-abuse. But I still had more anger. I was angry this was happening to me. It seemed beyond unfair. I have fought for good health all my adult life because I have had to. And I have ZERO cancer in my family history.

My reproductive profile put me at low risk. I was NOT supposed to be the one with cancer. I'd even written a book titled "Heal Thyself," for goodness sakes. Cancer and me? NO! It was as if I had a week to process the mountain of anger that I had been feeling for everything that was out of my control. I felt anger that my children and other family and friends would feel pain and anguish over my condition. I hated that I would be the cause of any of their suffering. I let myself feel the anger and fear. And I needed it. I processed it alone, in silence. And when that anger was gone, I could see the dim light of something new coming in, although I couldn't identify it yet.

January 7, 2021, was a surreal day. I wore one of my favorite outfits from my boutique, and I looked amazing. This gave me a sense of power and control over my life. As I floated along the OHSU halls with my husband on my arm, I felt a tiny glimmer of peace. I knew I had cancer. I knew I was being guided. As I went into the Breast Clinic and had a diagnostic mammogram, I engaged with the staff in a cheerful but authentic way. For their part, they seemed to be treating me delicately, as it was obvious, they were concerned by what they saw.

Following the mammogram, they sent me directly to an ultrasound, which only heightened their concern. We then were escorted to a waiting room where a kind, older doctor came in and spoke with us lightheartedly. It felt good to be in the care of a team now. I had waited over a month and a half, feeling very alone. In a way, being approved for state insurance at this perfect time made me feel as if God had not, in fact, abandoned me, and I said, "I see what you did there, God. Thank you." The doctor never used the word "cancer," and I think I was ready to hear it. I asked him, "If it's not cancer, then what is it?" He said, "The only other reasons [for the lumps] would be recent blunt trauma or diabetes." I remember feeling confused because we knew neither of those was the case.

On January 8th, I had a biopsy, which definitely was not pleasant. I had consented to allow a student doctor to perform the procedure, but the tumors were very hard to puncture, so the teaching doctor had to get more aggressive. I don't regret the student doctor's involvement. In fact, as a 22-year homeschool veteran of four, it was special for me to be part of a teaching opportunity. They placed markers by the tumors, and I was done for the day. My husband was a little shaken from watching the ordeal, but we gathered ourselves and walked out of the cancer center. Me - in a cancer center - it still didn't seem real.

I had several days to realize the doctor's answer to my question meant that it was, indeed, cancer. They were not doing a biopsy to see if it was cancer. The biopsy would simply tell them what type. As I did my best to keep our grown children, parents, and close friends informed, I pictured myself bald. I pictured myself dead. I'm really at ease with death; I know where I am going. But THIS was unacceptable. Making my adult children go through the rest of their lives without a mother was absolutely unacceptable. Widowing my sweet husband was unacceptable. My fear began to make way for a fierce determination to live. I absolutely would not leave my children, because I knew how important having me in their lives had been and will continue to be. They may not know it at ages 17-27, but I know they would feel the pain of my absence at their weddings, the births of their children, and every struggle in life when they just wanted to call on their mom. I was determined not to leave them.

A buying trip for our boutique took my 20-year-old daughter, Faith, and me to Dallas, Texas. I carefully considered if this was the right time to go, as I would be getting the biopsy results while there. But then, I knew it was cancer. We all agreed that because the boutique was the only real work joy I had in my life at that point, I should go. It was at 5 pm, after a very long and tiring day of shopping at The Dallas Market on January 13th, that the call came in. We were on the ground floor in the central atrium, and I found an empty table and sat down. Faith sat across from me and stared her giant eyes intently penetrating me, to read my eyes and listen as the kind nurse on the other end said, "invasive ductal carcinoma." I had one carcinoma measuring 3cm x 2.5cm, and another nearby carcinoma measuring 1.4cm x 1.3cm. These sat within a larger mass of suspicious tissue totaling an area of roughly 9.5cm at its largest dimension. There was an additional suspicious mass at the base of the right breast and also one in the left breast. As I responded to the nurse, I could see my beautiful Faith's eyes well up with tears and her chin quiver. The nurse said the biopsy confirmed a grade of 2 out of 3, and I took comfort that on the scale of aggressiveness, it wasn't a 3. She said it was ER+, PR+, and HER2-, and told me this is the most common and most treatable type. Okay, I have breast cancer and it is the best type to have. Got it.

The nurse said the OHSU Breast Clinic generally no longer recommends chemo for this type of cancer, and they also don't stage it because it is very treatable. She said they feel breast cancer has been over-treated for many years and they were making some changes. I liked what I heard.

She said they were very confident in their ability to cure my cancer. Okay. I have cancer. They are confident. I am confident. Got it. She was taken aback by my readiness to accept this and my understanding. She asked if I was surprised. I said, "No; I knew it weeks before I got imaging." In truth, I was relieved somewhat by the call and diagnosis and her encouragement. She informed me that a patient navigator would be walking this path with me and guiding me in my appointments, and I would not be alone in this process. Got it. Check. Got to go now. Click.

As I hung up my phone, my beautiful Faith crumbled into sobs, and I pulled her into my arms and said, "Oh, baby, I am not going anywhere. I have a battle ahead of me, but I assure you, I am not leaving you. I've got this, and it is okay to cry, and it is okay to be mad, and it is okay to be anything you need to be. And it is absolutely okay to be scared."

Somehow, we made the long walk back to our hotel room, but I don't remember it. I sat down and realized that I not only had the tough job of making calls, but I also had to make them in front of my daughter. It occurred to me to send her down for some food from the restaurant. That allowed me to make the first and toughest call – the one to my husband. "Hi," I said. "Hi," he replied. I managed to choke out with as much strength as I could fake, "It's cancer." I had already explained to him that it was, and the biopsy would just be giving us more information. He tried to stifle and hide any tears. I don't even remember any dialogue after that except telling him the good things. It's the most common type - over 3/4ths of all breast cancer is this - and the doctors are very confident and even said I won't be recommended for chemo. He and I already knew we would be the least likely candidates to take a western approach to cancer, and I would most likely refuse chemo, even if strongly recommended. So, it felt like that was a battle I wouldn't have to fight.

Following my call to my husband, I informed each of my parents and felt my heartbreak over the pain I was causing them. At this point, my Faith returned to me. (No, the double meaning when I use her name is never lost on me). It was time to call my other children. My children are all close, having grown up home-schooled together. First, we called Jonah, our 22-year-old Marine, because he would be going down for the night the soonest. Then, we called 17-year-old Grace, and then 27-year-old Austin. The strength I had to muster to speak this awful news to each child, in the presence of another child, never will be forgotten. It broke my heart to cause them any fear, pain, or anguish. Hearing the choked-back tears broke my heart and I vowed once again to conquer cancer.

As my daughter and I ate in our room, we polished off a good amount of wine together and enjoyed more tears, as well as more than a few laughs. We managed to get some sleep before our return home to Oregon, where everything was about to change ... again.

The process of accurately assessing what I was facing blended together. Doctors thought I had a mass in the left breast, too, and I was sent for more imaging and biopsy. Thankfully, they didn't find anything. I had another area of concern on the right breast, but they didn't biopsy that. I was presented with the option to do a lumpectomy, a single mastectomy, or a double mastectomy. I asked about which of those would reduce the odds of them recommending radiation. At this point, I wanted to work within both their comfort zone and mine. I knew I did not want to irradiate my body. They said lumpectomy with radiation has the same outcome as a double mastectomy without radiation. I chose a double mastectomy. They tried to talk me out of it, but I said, "Look, I have all kinds of suspicious-looking tissue all over in these things and quite literally, I'm done with them. I breastfed for a collective 7 years and had 5 babies (I was a gestational surrogate), and they still misbehaved. Have away with them. I'm done."

The team wanted me to be on hormone blockers to block estrogen until my surgery. Fine. It's a short time, and I don't want this stuff to have a chance to spread either. The side effects of Tamoxifen made me feel awful. After just a month on it, I knew I would decline to take it for the 5-10 years they were recommending. I had my Oncotype run and my number was only a 3 (that is if they found no cancer in my lymph nodes at surgery, and if I took Tamoxifen. If there was cancer in my lymph nodes, then my score would be 11.) I spoke with my team about this, and it just supported everyone's shock that I even had breast cancer. I asked about my chance of reoccurrence if I did NOT take the hormone blockers. They informed me the chance of recurrence would double. I said, "So, you are telling me this drug is reducing my risk of recurrence by 3% in exchange for horrible side effects and increased risk of uterine cancer?" Yep. "Well, that doesn't sound like a smart exchange in my book," I informed them. "How much does keeping my nipples increase my risk of recurrence?" I asked. The doctor replied, "Yeah, it's about that much." "So, you are saying that percentage-wise, the hormone blockers and removing my nipples with the mastectomy carry about the same protection?", I clarified? "Yes," replied the oncologist. "All right then, we have a plan. Take my nipples, because; I'm not taking your drug," I stated. He looked at me wide-eyed. I don't know if it was because he thought I was brilliant, bold, or stupid, but that was my answer.

At the same time, all of this was happening, my husband's rising PSA had taken a giant leap, and he agreed to a repeat MRI to check for cancer. (He'd had an MRI the previous February, and doctors had said his prostate was clear.) Because of our health concerns, we embarked on a 42-day cancer-specific fast (we are experienced fasters) that started us out on vegetable broth (up to two cups per day) and a special vegetable juice recipe (up to two cups per day), with the goal as the fast progressed of taking in as little of this as possible. We quickly progressed to just a few mouthfuls each a day. We embarked on the fast in February, and I made it 30 days. My husband did the full 42. I carefully grilled my team about how much, if any, a tumor could shrink while on Tamoxifen alone, and they confirmed that it will not shrink at all. The Tamoxifen is taken to hopefully stabilize and prevent metastasis. At the end of my 30- day fast, my pre-surgery imaging showed a decrease in tumor size. Nevertheless, I knew I couldn't outlast my tumors by fasting. One can only fast so much, for so long. I knew my breasts were expendable, so I planned to go forward with the surgery. I was hopeful the fast had gotten my husband some good results, and even if it didn't make us cancer-free, it definitely made us healthier.

When I was diagnosed with cancer, I had a meeting with my daughters and husband and said, "Look, my top priority is going to be fighting cancer and recovering. I am going to need you all to step up in these three businesses and help keep them going. But if they fail; that is Okay. We are okay." The process of letting go, and the inner work I was required to do during this seemingly endless time, was causing amazing results for me. I was able to reach a place of happiness I had never known as an adult. I felt free and it was weird. I was walking around happy and fighting cancer and it was surreal. I still couldn't believe it.

On March 16th, 2021, I went into the hospital for my double mastectomy. Once again, I had to defend my choice for a non-nipple-sparing double mastectomy. I explained I was trusting the lead of the Holy Spirit, my gut, my inner voice, and my intuition. I had been very logical about my choices and risks and made my own choices about what risks I was willing to take. I wanted reconstruction because I was only 47, love fashion and dressing up, and also hate bras.

Thus, reconstruction was a no-brainer for me. If implants made me sick or went wrong, I could always go flat.

In the surgery, the doctors got clear margins and my lymph nodes were clear, so radiation was up to me. My husband and I prayed about it, and I chose to forgo radiation. Coming out of the surgery and hearing that my lymph nodes were clear was a big win for us. The clear margin thing took more time to confirm. My operative notes suggested margins were not clear, so we had to get confirmation from the surgeon that they were, in fact, clear.

Due to my underlying health conditions of adrenal insufficiency, ataxia, and dystonia, I had a very hard time at the hospital. My recovery was slow and bumpy, but I was okay. I had a flat, ugly, cellophaned chest with markers and incisions and three drains. Family and friends sent flowers, and I cannot express how good that made me feel. I felt frustrated that only a couple of meals were provided to us during this time, but I also understood that due to my husband's and my health status and our chosen plant-based diet, many people didn't have the confidence to provide us with appropriate food. Nevertheless, because I am a freaking handful after surgery and my family was trying to keep our businesses going, it would have been really great to have some help with meals. I bring this up to recommend to others deciding whether to send flowers or gifts to SEND FOOD! It likely will get eaten and if it doesn't, it still will provide a valuable feeling of love.

April came along with me recovering and getting expansions of my newly mutilated chest, and it was time for that MRI for my husband. We were nervous because it was taking longer than we thought it should to hear from the doctor with the results. When the call finally came a week later, I sensed unease in the words the doctor was choosing. I had the overwhelming sense that something wasn't right about what he was saying. He said he was waiting for the imaging center from the previous year to get back to him and confirm what he was seeing had not been visible on the images 15 months earlier. There was a large mass on my husband's sacrum suspicious of a sacrococcygeal chordoma, a rare bone cancer. Focused imaging would be required for confirmation. We were shaken. The doctor hung up and I threw my arms around my husband; fully intending to whisper words of encouragement, but all I could do was cry. I wanted to say something strong and encouraging, but I couldn't even speak. My GOD, now I was scared! My life - no problem. My husband's? Living without him was NOT an option.

He finally got an imaging appointment at a small center that did a spine-based MRI, which confirmed he had a rapidly growing chordoma when compared to imaging from last year. LAST YEAR?! We called and said they must be mistaken; the doctor had said it wasn't visible on those images. It took three days for the imaging center to get back to us and confirm that the chordoma was, in fact, visible on the previous images. I obtained copies of the previous images, installed medical imaging software, and took a look for myself. I'm not a medical professional, but I own a yoga school and have taught anatomy to teachers.

Even a total newbie to anatomy could see a mass that shouldn't be there on the images from 15 months earlier.

The shock, the anger, and the fear were overwhelming. It was as though I'd been sent on a treacherous, painful climb dealing with my breast cancer, and I made it to the top of that mountain. But just as I arrived at the precipice and stretched my arms in triumphant victory, I turned around and a mountain 100 times larger stood before me. I was consumed by the injustice and unfairness of it. I was enraged that the doctors had missed this and not informed us 15 months earlier.

Chordoma is a rare bone cancer that comes from leftover fetal cells that form the spinal cord, but then decide to become cancerous. It does not respond to chemo. It does not respond to radiation. The only recommended course of treatment is en bloc resection (i.e., complete removal of the tumor with clear margins of healthy tissue surrounding it) and proton therapy, in that order. In other words, they amputate the base of the spine. The neurological deficits would be great, and life-changing. Our lives went into a tailspin as we sought out consults around the country, ultimately flying to MD Anderson in Houston.

My husband chose to embark on every holistic healing path he could find as we closely monitored the size of the tumor every 3 months with an MRI. Somehow, I managed to settle into trusting that God was directing this entire, horrible show, and even my husband's mindset was in God's control. I reached depths of hopelessness and despair I cannot explain adequately with words.

On August 2nd, I went in for my exchange surgery and had implants with fat grafting placed. Again, I had post-surgical complications with adrenal insufficiency and adrenal crisis as well as my movement disorders, but we managed, and obviously, I lived, so that was good. The "foobs" looked good, all things considered. I didn't care about them. Me, my health, and my foobs were overshadowed (in my mind) by my husband's cancer, and the great lengths we were taking to explore alternative therapies, healing-specific juicing, food prep, and eating. I had no space to care about my stupid chest. The weight of trying to fight his cancer ourselves was suffocating what little life I had left in me, and it was suffocating him, too.

It was during this deep, dark point that Deb Hart reached out to me. As a business owner and author in the healing fields, I am accustomed to constant solicitation from direct sales reps with enthusiasm that I am their next big close. So, when I saw the message from Deb that just said, "Call me", I thought, "Yeah, right." But then I heard a still, small voice that said, "Yes; call her." I did, and I'm so glad I did. As a woman who had been very driven, strong, self-sufficient, and fearless (not to mention having alternative views), I also chose my company carefully. I didn't see myself as someone who would want to go to a 'support group.' Deb didn't want to sell me anything. She wanted to offer me a chance to step out of my circumstances for an afternoon and just have some fun. What?! Fun? What is that? I told her I would love to have fun, but I was broker than broke. She said, "Oh, that is the best part; it's a gift to you. You don't pay a thing." I might have cried silently. I was in.

So, I went to the marina not knowing what to expect. I explained that I was a hot freaking mess, only 4 weeks out of reconstruction surgery, not able to get in water yet, and with a movement disorder that could make even walking around the dock with moving water in my peripheral vision difficult. No problem. Come on down and have fun! Being able to sit with a group of women who had been going through the crisis of breast cancer was amazing. We took some time to share our stories, and that was when I fell apart with the freshness and terror of my husband's cancer in my heart. I didn't know how to say, "Hey, my BC was horrible, but it is nothing compared to this. I'm paralyzed. I don't even know what to do." But I received love and support and it was a salve for my soul. We went over to a small island called McGuire Island (which excited me because I have always joked about claiming that island as mine since that is my last name). Once there, we sat in the sun and visited and laughed. Some of us shared our scars and our stories, and it felt good to hold each other's space, with zero pity in sight.

I left the event feeling better than I had in months. And when I returned to my car, I received a message from my Marine son on deployment, telling me I was going to be a grandma! I tell you, my heart almost exploded. I knew I could cling to what I was feeling that day to pull myself out of the deep, dark despair of hopelessness I had been drowning in.

We have continued to experience struggles since that day. The ongoing difficulties from Covid, my husband's continuing battle with his cancer, his mother's death from Covid, my ER visits due to a kidney stone, and bouts of adrenal insufficiency. Nevertheless, I am rallying. I'm remembering I can choose to be all right. I can even choose to be happy. And my life is changing in beautiful ways that could never be so without all the struggles we've faced. Our story isn't finished yet, but we look forward to looking back on this tough span of years with a new appreciation for life and happiness. Admittedly, we should like to not climb another mountain for a very long time.

Tara L. McGuire

Tara is an author and activist in the fields of health, healing, self-improvement, and empowered birth. As owner and operator of a holistic health spa, a yoga center, and a yoga school, she has flexed her entrepreneurial muscle to be able to home school her four children for 22 years.

Married to her best friend and business partner, Don Marthaller, they collectively devour alternative and complementary practices for health and healing in their Gresham, Oregon-based home. Having authored Birth Unhindered and Heal Thyself, Tara looks forward to pushing into semi-retirement and spending more time authoring books that will inspire and empower people in their paths to live healthier, happier lives.

Retired from child-rearing, her and her husband have been focusing the last two years on fighting the business ramifications of COVID, the total impact of her breast cancer, and her husband's rare bone cancer. Their story is engaging and evolving and they invite you to follow them at #taraanddoncancerjourney and #prayfordonm on social platforms.

Connect with Tara:
taramcguire@mac.com
FB @TaraLynnMcGuire
IG @TaraLynnMcGuire

WAVE AFTER WAVE OF PINK

The Many Revelations of "The Big C"

April Everist

I'm in the room, you know the one, all survivors do. It is white with a bed and an ultrasound machine. In the middle of this room, one of the ceiling panels has been switched out with a photo installation. The scene has fluffy clouds and blue skies. More importantly, this is the room where my world would soon be turned upside down.

When I changed into my gown on that warm day in late September. I thought to myself how nice it must be for those receiving bad news to have something comforting to look at. I remember being that person as I looked up at the panel when I heard the radiologist say to me that they believed my suspicious lump was cancer. All I could do in that moment was fixate on the word "cancer" and surrender to the needle now pointed in my direction plunging me and the life I once knew into a new trajectory.

My life prior to that day, as my mother would say, was a charmed one. A single, well-educated, outgoing, 33-year-old with a thriving career. I was in excellent health as an organic eater, fitness fanatic, and a near-daily meditator. Aside from enjoying a glass of wine and having a sweet tooth, I was by most standards, living a healthy lifestyle.

Unlike many breast cancer symptoms, pain is what drew me to the lump. I went to favor my left breast one summer morning that previous August and felt the small nodular. This is new, I thought. I convinced myself that it was probably a harmless cyst, like one I had experienced before in my late teens. Given my age, the thought that my lump could be cancer was the last thing on my mind. As a result, I ignored it and told myself that it would go away just like the other cyst had in the past. Luckily, the slight twinge persisted over the next few weeks. Intuitively, I knew the pain was telling me something wasn't right. By mid-September, I had made an appointment with my primary care physician, setting my mentioned path above into motion.

In the few agonizing days that it took to get my biopsy results, fear consumed me. In a free fall of my emotions and desperate to grasp onto any control, I began to research. I had to know everything about breast cancer, from the best prognosis to the worst, assessing all the various treatment options and outcomes for each. In those few days everything that I'd read terrified me. The reality that my life was about to significantly change had set in.

Faced with the immediacy of my death, all the fears and insecurities that I'd had prior to my diagnosis, felt menial in comparison. Feeling at my most vulnerable, I began to question my mortality and specifically if I would die from this disease. I clung to my phone, as I broke the news to my family and close friends. I knew I was going to need all the support I could get in order to survive what was ahead of me.

When my biopsy results came in, I was initially told that my lump was Ductal Carcinoma in Situ (DCIS). Which is a noninvasive pre-cancer. At the time, this was a huge relief. However, after my first surgery, a lumpectomy, the pathology results discovered that in the center of my 1.9cm DCIS tumor, was 5mm of invasive cancer. Furthermore, the pathology report indicated the grade three tumor was triple positive (ER+/PR+/HER2+). Unfortunately, this meant another surgery to remove more breast tissue and lymph nodes.

My diagnosis was upstaged to T1A (no lymph node involvement). Just prior to my second procedure, I received a call from my surgeon indicating that upon review of my case, the oncology team would be recommending chemotherapy and targeted therapy. With this critical information, I reluctantly agreed to have a port catheter placed just below my right collar bone. When I thought of chemotherapy, my mind could only think about the extremely scary side effects (severe nausea, vomiting, rapid weight, and hair loss) that are dramatized in movies and television. In this reflection, I realized that all of my opinions of chemotherapy and cancer treatments were rooted in these fears.

Naturally, I dreaded and resisted the idea that I would need conventional treatments. My anxiety heightened when I thought about receiving the "poison". I obsessed about all the things that could go wrong during the treatment process. I feared all of the harsh side effects but also knew the treatments would destroy cancer cells. At a stalemate, I decided that I would not let my fears of treatment stop me from a recommended plan, especially if it could save my life.

During the first appointment with my oncologist, I was surprised to hear how far cancer treatment had come. I learned there were different types of chemotherapy and cancer targeting treatments, many of which were tolerable enough for patients to continue with their daily routines. Also, breast radiation was unlikely to make me severely ill, nor would it contribute to more head-hair loss. My oncologist even informed me of a process called cold capping, where many cancer patients were successfully maintaining more than half of their hair while undergoing chemotherapy!

This appointment was a pivotal turning point for me. It is important for me to acknowledge that not every plan and response to treatment is the same, however, I realized that much of my knowledge of chemotherapy and other cancer treatments was completely uninformed and misguided. Especially since I would receive a tolerable course of 12 weeks of Paclitaxel, 18 rounds of targeted therapy, and short-course radiation. To my surprise, instead of feeling powerless, my treatment plan gave me hope. For the first time since my diagnosis, I finally felt a sense of control over my body.

Feeling empowered, I sprang into action and put several things in place a few weeks before my first infusion. I saw a naturopathic doctor who specialized in cancer care and recommended many complementing remedies (confirming that they would not interfere with conventional treatment). I strictly adhered to a ketogenic diet and started experimenting with intermittent fasting. Most excitingly, I ordered a cold cap system, in an attempt to save my hair! Then, I rallied up my family and friends to assist me on infusion days. With all of the preparation, I was ready to embrace my biggest fear on this journey.

Prior to the first treatment, the subject of preserving my fertility weighed heavily on my mind and heart. I knew in my twenties that I wanted to be a mother someday. I often daydreamed of a little girl whose features and mannerisms resembled my own. However, my circumstances up to my diagnosis hadn't presented the opportunity yet. After discussing the topic with my oncologist, I opted to get a monthly injection, which would protect my reproductive system during treatment. I continue to remain on this injection, in addition to an oral aromatase inhibitor, until my five-year marker. All in the hopes that my fertility will return and prevent the chance of recurrence.

Infusion days, to my surprise, weren't nearly as scary as I had built them up to be. Other than a slight poke to access my port, the actual infusions themselves, were painless and uneventful. Additionally, with the help of pre-treatment medications and acupuncture, I never had to hug the porcelain throne. Also, the cold caps proved to be a huge success, as I ended my last chemotherapy infusion with a full head of hair!

Now, I don't want to diminish the side effects of chemotherapy for anyone. The experience is different for each patient. I still suffered from many unpleasant ones, but as each week passed without any complications, I began to grow more confident and less fearful of the treatment process.

As strange as it sounds, what I valued most while going through cancer treatments was how much closer it brought me to my family and friends. I fondly reflect back as each loved one took turns meticulously strapping my cold cap onto my head during infusion days. They'd tuck me in on the couch, to watch shows or play games, as we enjoyed the keto-approved meals that they had prepared for me. From the support of my employer and coworkers rooting me on to all the messages of well wishes. I greatly attribute all of those supportive efforts to the acceleration of my healing, both physically and emotionally.

Throughout the year of my journey, a string of unfortunate events happened within my family. Two of my grandparents passed away. Additionally, my step-mother, a metastatic stage IV breast cancer survivor herself, had a cancerous tumor return. And to boot, just four months after my diagnosis, my maternal grandmother was also diagnosed with breast cancer. This, despite both of us testing negative for any BRCA mutations. I'm happy to share that they have both recovered. However, my cancer alone would have been challenging enough, but experiencing the loss of loved ones and also watching those you care about suffer from the same disease was more crisis than anyone typically experiences in the span of a year.

As I navigated through these moments of hardship, I knew that at some point I wanted to connect to a group of survivors in some way. When one enters the world of disease, you enter into a community of people that get it. They are there for you in a way only the sick and surviving can be. It was exactly what I needed at just the right time, when my former college roommate's mother connected me to Pink Sistas, for a no-cost weekend retreat with other survivors of breast cancer.

When I arrived at the retreat home on the river, the gracious Pink Sistas Founder greeted me and ensured that I felt at ease. After meeting each survivor and having one of the many delicious meals made for us, we gathered and shared our stories. We gave each other tips and advice on the remedies that worked for our treated bodies. During the weekend I could flop and flail around without any judgment during all the physical activities (yoga, water sports, boat rides). I didn't get any puzzled looks when I frantically stripped off layers of clothing during a hot flash. We would even reach a place of sacred trust to show each other the scars and outcomes from our surgeries. In our shared comradery of survivorship, we understood each other and could be our authentic selves.

The Pink Sistas weekend gave me the time to reflect on the enormity of what I endured since the day of my diagnosis. As this chapter is so titled, I have had many revelations while on this journey. Many of which you have just read. Cancer undoubtedly has been the most challenging and difficult time of my life, but it has also been the most impactful and transformational.

I have a whole new perspective and passion for life because of this experience. I chase my dreams, leap into new challenges, and dive headfirst into every day. I have developed into one of the best and healthiest versions of myself through this journey.

Cancer has inspired me to embrace my fears and transform them into what I need to persevere in the moment. I am no longer held back by the fear of if or when I might die from this disease. I am completely unburdened and I am finally free from cancer.

April attended Western Oregon University and graduated with a Bachelor of Science Degree in Criminal Justice.

Professionally, April is a Victim Services Coordinator for a law enforcement agency and assists survivors of domestic violence and sexual assault. However, at the age of 33, April was faced with a shocking diagnosis of triple-positive breast cancer. With the need to advocate for herself, April endured two surgeries, chemotherapy, targeted therapy, and radiation. April balanced both conventional treatment and naturopathic methods, in addition to successfully retaining her hair with cold cap therapy. Through the support of April's medical team, family, and friends, April is now cancer-free.

Connect with April:
Email: april_everist@outlook.com

My Metastatic Breast Cancer Journey!

Christine Terry

I am Christine Terry, 58 years old, and live in Vancouver WA. I was diagnosed with metastatic breast cancer in April 2019, almost six years from the day of my original breast cancer diagnosis.

Initial Diagnosis and Treatment

In 2013, my 14-year marriage was struggling, taking care of three kids, I was working too many hours in Portland to keep my head above water in a job that exceeded my skill set, and I was taking Humaira, an immune suppressor for psoriatic arthritis, ankylosing spondylitis, and Crohn's disease.

During spring break in 2013, I felt a lump in my breast and it turned out to be Stage II HER2-, HR + breast cancer. I immediately went on short-term disability, and underwent neoadjuvant care of chemotherapy, followed by a double mastectomy.

I made light of the situation, joking about being 'perky' for the rest of my life, embracing 'survivorship' and all the rah-rah that goes along with that. There was nothing funny about my situation.

I tried to maintain my marriage, take care of my kids, keep up with housework, go back to the office and continue my passion; cycling.

I had reconstruction in December 2013, and 2014 was one of the most difficult years of my life. My husband and I were working on a divorce, rather than recovering from breast cancer treatment. Our divorce was final on March 4, 2015. I said that I will "March Forth'" as I tried to turn a major disappointment into a positive.

Post Cancer

Given those challenges and stress, I thought that's why I got breast cancer and I considered cancer was 'one and done'.

For the next five years, I focused on myself, kids, home, community, and work. I took on a new role at work, helped my daughter to college, focused on my boys graduating high school, worked on trail maintenance at Whipple Creek Regional Park, and cycled as much as I could!

Oh yes, I got a dog too! – Bebe, who saved my soul!

Cancer has my Attention

In the fall of 2018, I was extremely fatigued, my blood pressure was suddenly through the roof and I could barely breathe pedaling up a small hill on the road!

The oncologists could not find anything in terms of cancer recurrence, blood work was normal, cancer markers were normal, no headaches, etc.

Thank God my dermatologist found a melanoma patch on my arm! As the surgeon was removing stitches from my arm, I hesitantly mentioned a tight muscle in my neck. He ordered an ultrasound and, BAM!!!, there was breast cancer in my lymph nodes, spine, other bones, and lungs. The Metastatic Breast Cancer Journey begins.

Six months of chemotherapy cleared all the cancer except for my spine. I completely changed my lifestyle.... Organic whole foods, minimal dairy and processed foods, daily light exercise, community breast cancer support and I can now spell 'metastatic' without spellcheck!

I am grateful to my naturopathic oncologist who recommended two books, both of which changed my life:
1. Radical Remission by Kelly A. Turner
2. Cancer Fighting Kitchen Cookbook by Rebecca Katz

Cancer Community Support
Pink Lemonade Project:

I am forever grateful for The Pink Lemonade Project as their survivorship programs continue to assist me in recovery, physically and mentally. I also met and became friends with Penda Sidibeh, she is living with Metastatic Breast Cancer too and we support one another!

Legacy Health:
Incredible cancer survivor exercise and nutrition classes, as well as support groups.

Pink Sistas:
In the summer of 2021, the cancer drug side effects were very challenging for me, therefore, I took a 12-week leave of absence from work. This allowed me to participate in several Pink Sista retreats. Despite the pandemic, we warrior women got out there and enjoyed one another! You're an angel, Deb Hart!

Marching Forth
I am LIVING with metastatic breast cancer. I will continue to live every day doing what I love to do, with my 'person', Brooklyn!

Connect with Christine
Ph: 360-713-3099

WAVE AFTER WAVE OF PINK

How You Can Help?

Your donations allow us to do the good work that we do in educating, supporting, and creating community through no cost retreats for Breast Cancer fighters.

100%...

...of your donations go directly to supporting our programs and operations. Thank you for your support.

pinksistas.org/howyoucanhelp

GLOSSARY

ABRAXANE
Abraxane typically is used to treat advanced-stage breast cancer and usually is given in combination with other chemo- therapy medicines or after other chemotherapy medicines given after surgery have stopped working.

ALLODERM
Alloderm is a biologic mesh-like material derived from animals or donated (cadaveric) human skin. It is used in many different types of reconstructive surgery including breast reconstruction.

AROMATASE INHIBITOR
Aromatase inhibitors stop the production of estrogen in post-menopausal women. Aromatase inhibitors work by blocking the enzyme aromatase, which turns the hormone androgen into small amounts of estrogen in the body. This means that less estrogen is available to stimulate the growth of hormone-receptor-positive breast cancer cells.

ATYPICAL EPITHELIAL HYPERPLASIA
Atypical hyperplasia is a precancerous condition that affects cells in the breast. Atypical hyperplasia describes an accumulation of abnormal cells in the milk ducts and lobules of the breast. Atypical hyperplasia isn't cancer, but it increases the risk of breast cancer.

AXILLARY NODE DISSECTION
An axillary lymph node dissection (ALND) is surgery to remove lymph nodes from the armpit (underarm or axilla). The lymph nodes in the armpit are called axillary lymph nodes. An ALND is also called axillary dissection, axillary node dissection or axillary lymphadenectomy.

BIOPSY
A biopsy is a procedure to remove a piece of tissue or a sample of cells from your body so that it can be analyzed in a laboratory.

BRCA1 AND BRCA2 (BRCA1/2) GENE MUTATION
Genes that help limit cell growth. A mutation (change) in one of these genes increases a person's risk of breast, ovarian, and certain other cancers. Everyone has BRCA1 and BRCA2 genes.

CARCINOMA
Cancer that begins in the skin or in tissues that line or cover internal organs.

CHEMO BRAIN
A term commonly used to describe thinking and memory problems that a patient with cancer may have before, during, or after cancer treatment. Signs and symptoms of chemo brain include disorganized behavior or thinking, confusion, memory loss, and trouble concentrating, paying attention, learning, and making decisions. Chemo brain may be caused by the cancer itself (such as brain tumors) or by cancer treatment, such as chemotherapy and other anticancer drugs, radiation therapy, hormone therapy, and surgery. It may also be caused by conditions related to cancer treatment, such as anemia, fatigue, infection, pain, hormone changes, sleep problems, nutrition problems, stress, anxiety, and depression. Chemo brain may last for a short time or for many years.

CYTOXAN
Cytoxan (cyclophosphamide) is a cancer (chemotherapy) medication used to treat several types of cancer.

DIEP FLAP RECONSTRUCTION
A type of breast reconstruction procedure. During DIEP flap reconstruction surgery, a surgeon will take healthy tissue, skin, and fat from the person's lower abdomen to use in breast reconstruction.

DUCTAL CARCINOMA IN SITU
If cancers arise in the ducts of the breast (the tubes that carry milk to the nipple when a woman is breastfeeding) and do not grow outside of the ducts, the tumor is called ductal carcinoma in situ (DCIS). DCIS cancers do not spread beyond the breast tissue. However, DCIS may develop over time into invasive cancers if not treated.

EARLY BREAST CANCER
Cancer that is contained in the breast or has only spread to lymph nodes in the underarm area. This term is often used to describe Stage 1 and Stage 2 breast cancer.

ENCAPSULATED
Confined to a specific, localized area and surrounded by a thin layer of tissue.

EXCISIONAL BIOPSY
A surgical procedure in which an entire lump or suspicious area is removed for diagnosis. The tissue is then examined under a microscope.

HER2-POSITIVE (HER2+) BREAST CANCER
In about 20% of breast cancers, the cells make too much of a protein known as HER2 (Human Epidermal Growth Factor Receptor 2, HER2/neu, erbB2). These cancers tend to be aggressive and fast-growing.
HER2-negative (HER–) breast cancers have little or no HER2 protein. HER2-positive (HER+) breast cancers have a lot of HER2 protein. HER2+ tumors can be treated with HER2-targeted therapies, such as trastuzumab (Herceptin).

HER2 POSITIVE OR NEGATIVE
About 10% to 20% of breast cancers depend on the gene called human epidermal growth factor receptor 2 (HER2) to grow. These cancers are called "HER2 positive" and have too many HER2 receptors and/or extra copies of the HER2 gene. The HER2 gene makes a protein that is found on the cancer cell and is important for tumor cell growth. A breast cancer that does not have excessive numbers of HER2 receptors or copies of the HER2 gene is called "HER2 negative."

HERCEPTIN
A drug used alone or with other drugs to treat certain types of breast cancer, stomach cancer, and gastroesophageal junction cancer that are HER2 positive. It is also being studied in the treatment of other types of cancer. Herceptin binds to a protein called HER2, which is found on some cancer cells. This may help the immune system kill cancer cells. Herceptin is a type of monoclonal antibody and a type of HER2 receptor antagonist.

HORMONE RECEPTOR POSITIVE OR NEGATIVE
Breast cancers expressing estrogen receptors (ER) and progesterone receptors (PR) are called "hormone receptor positive." These cancers may depend on the hormone's estrogen and/or progesterone to grow. A breast cancer that does not have estrogen and progesterone receptors is called "hormone receptor negative".

INFLAMMATORY BREAST CANCER (IBC)
A rare, aggressive form of invasive breast cancer whose main symptoms are swelling (inflammation) and redness of the breast. The skin on the breast may look dimpled, like the skin of an orange, and may be warm to the touch.

INVASIVE DUCTAL CARCINOMA (IDC)
IDC, also known as infiltrating ductal carcinoma, is cancer that began growing in a milk duct and has invaded the fibrous or fatty tissue of the breast outside of the duct. IDC is the most common form of breast cancer, representing eighty percent of all breast cancer diagnoses.

LI-FRAUMENI SYNDROME (LFS)
Li-Fraumeni syndrome (LFS) is an inherited familial predisposition to a wide range of certain, often rare, cancers. This is due to a change (mutation) in a tumor suppressor gene known as TP53. The resulting p53 protein produced by the gene is damaged (or otherwise rendered malfunctioning), and is unable to help prevent malignant tumors from developing.
Individuals with LFS have an approximately 50% of developing cancer by age 40, and up to a 90% percent chance by age 60, while females have nearly a 100% risk of developing cancer in their lifetime due to their markedly increased risk of breast cancer. Many individuals with LFS develop two or more primary cancers over their lifetimes.

LUMPECTOMY (BREAST CONSERVING SURGERY)
Breast surgery that removes only the tumor and a small rim of normal tissue around it, leaving most of the breast skin and tissue in place.

MARGINS
The rim of normal tissue surrounding a tumor that's removed during breast surgery.
A margin is clean (also known as uninvolved, negative or clear) if there's only normal tissue (and no cancer cells) at the edges. Clean margins show the entire tumor was removed.
With involved (positive) margins, normal tissue doesn't completely surround the tumor. This means the entire tumor was not removed and more surgery may be needed to get clean margins.

MASTECTOMY
Surgical removal of the breast. The exact procedure depends on the diagnosis.

METASTASES
If any cancer is detectable outside of the breast, these deposits are called metastases.

METASTATIC BREAST CANCER
Breast cancer that has spread beyond the breast to other organs in the body (most often the bones, lungs, liver or brain).

Metastatic breast cancer is not a specific type of breast cancer, but rather the most advanced stage (Stage 4) of breast cancer.

N.E.D.
No evidence of disease (NED) is often used with cancer when there is no physical evidence of the disease on examination or imaging tests after treatment. No evidence of disease means the same thing as complete remission or complete response. It does not, however, mean that a cancer is cured.

NEULASTA
A drug that is used to prevent infection in adults and children with neutropenia (a lower-than-normal number of white blood cells) caused by anticancer drugs that may stop or slow the growth of blood-forming cells in the bone marrow. Neulasta helps the bone marrow make more white blood cells.

NEUTROPENIA
Neutropenia is when a person has a low level of neutrophils. Neutrophils are a type of white blood cell. All white blood cells help the body fight infection. Neutrophils fight infection by destroying harmful bacteria and fungi (yeast) that invade the body.

ONOCTYPE SCORE
The Oncotype DX test is a genomic test that analyzes the activity of a group of twenty-one genes from a breast cancer tissue sample that can affect how a cancer is likely to behave and respond to treatment.

OOPHORECTOMY
Surgery to remove one or both ovaries.

PERI MENOPAUSE
Peri menopause, or menopause transition, begins several years before menopause. It's the time when the ovaries gradually begin to make less

estrogen. It usually starts in women's 40s, but can start in their 30's or even earlier.

PERJETA
A drug used with other drugs to treat HER2 positive breast cancer. It is used in patients whose cancer has spread to other parts of the body and has not already been treated with other anticancer drugs. It is also used before surgery in patients with locally advanced, inflammatory, or early-stage breast cancer and after surgery in patients with early-stage breast cancer who have a high risk that their cancer will recur (come back). It is also being studied in the treatment of other types of cancer. Perjeta binds to a protein called HER2, which is found on some cancer cells. Blocking this protein may help kill cancer cells.

PET SCAN
A Positron Emission Tomography (PET) scan is an imaging test that helps reveal how your tissues and organs are functioning. A PET scan uses a radioactive drug (tracer) to show this activity.

A PET scan is useful in revealing or evaluating several conditions, including many cancers, heart disease and brain disorders. Often, PET images are combined with CT or MRI scans to create special views.

PROPHYLACTIC MASTECTOMY
Surgery to remove one or both breasts to reduce the risk of developing breast cancer. According to the National Cancer Institute, prophylactic mastectomy in women who carry a BRCA1 or BRCA2 gene mutation may be able to reduce the risk of developing breast cancer by 95%.

STAGE 0
This stage describes cancer in situ, which means "in place." Stage 0 cancers are still located in the place they started and have not spread to nearby tissues. This stage of cancer is often highly curable, usually by removing the entire tumor with surgery.

STAGE I
This stage is usually a small cancer or tumor that has not grown deeply into nearby tissues. It also has not spread to the lymph nodes or other parts of the body. It is often called early-stage cancer.

STAGE II AND III
In general, these 2 stages indicate larger cancers or tumors that have grown more deeply into nearby tissue. They may have also spread to lymph nodes but not to other parts of the body.

STAGE IV
This stage means that the cancer has spread to other organs or parts of the body. It may also be called advanced or metastatic cancer.

TAMOXIFEN (NOLVADEX)
A hormone therapy drug (taken in pill form) used to treat early and advanced stage breast cancers that are hormone receptor- positive. These breast cancers need estrogen to grow. Tamoxifen stops or slows the growth of these tumors by blocking estrogen from attaching to hormone receptors in the cancer cells.

TAXOL
Taxol is an anti-cancer ("antineoplastic" or "cytotoxic") chemo- therapy drug. Taxol is classified as a "plant alkaloid," a "taxane" and an "antimicrotubule agent."

TISSUE EXPANDERS
Tissue expanders are temporary, empty implants that are gradually inflated with saline over time. This stretches the skin (and muscle if the expander is placed under the muscle) to make room for the breast implants.

TRIPLE NEGATIVE BREAST CANCER
A breast cancer that is estrogen receptor-negative, progesterone receptor-negative and HER2-negative. This type of breast cancer may grow more quickly than hormone receptor-positive disease, and chemotherapy may work better as a treatment. Inflammatory breast cancer is often triple negative.

VENA CAVA
A large vein that carries blood to the heart from other areas of the body. The vena cava has two parts: the superior vena cava and the inferior vena cava. The superior vena cava carries blood from the head, neck, arms, and chest. The inferior vena cava carries blood from the legs, feet, and organs in the abdomen and pelvis. The vena cava is the largest vein in the body.

Acknowledgements

We truly appreciate these amazing sponsors that donate their services to help us continue our no-cost day retreats. Pink Sistas retreats wouldn't be what they are today without their help, so we ask you to please show them some love!

FRED MEYER

Weston Kia

Stevens Marine

Pepsi-Cola Columbia Distributing

Sextant Bar and Galley